MW01074986

LIVE IN FAITH:

From Islam to Christ

By Max Tahtamouni

xulon
PRESS

LIVE IN FAITH: From Islam to Christ
by Max Tahtamouni

Printed in the United States of America

ISBN 9781626976726

www.xulonpress.com

Acknowledgement

I would like to thank first and give all glory to the Lord for His blessings and miracles in bringing us through a terrible time. I also want to thank my pastors, John from Living Word and Lynndene from House of Prayer, and our respective church families; my father-in-law and mother-in-law, David and Shirley; my father, sister and brothers; Agnes from the north, the friends who stood by me, my attorneys and my editor. I thank my wife for standing by my side every hour of the day over the past two years, my children for loving me and supporting me when their lives were turned upside down, and a special thanks to my eldest daughter, Änna, who strongly encouraged me, believed in me and fought for me.

Foreword

*B*ecause of legal and personal issues that were still unresolved at the time of publication, the names of many people involved in this story, as well as the names of cities, businesses, and organizations, have been changed or left out completely.

While the author's given name is *Muhannad*, his American nickname is *Max*.

Muhannad's Background

My name is Muhannad Tahtamouni. I was born in Jordan to Palestinian parents, Abdulrahim and Aisha. My father and mother were from the ancient biblical city of Beit Sean (*Besan* in Arabic). Their parents and ancestors originally came to Palestine from the Egyptian village of Tahtamoun nearly 500 years ago and this is where our name comes from.

In May 1948, when Israel was established as a nation, our relative, Jamal Tahtamouni, a general in the British army, told the Tahtamouni family to leave Besan. When Jamal advised the family to leave, he guaranteed them safe return back to Besan within three to four weeks. The Tahtamouni family and extended family listened to his recommendation, left the city within two to three days, crossed the Jordan River, and camped on the other side. Jamal was killed (we are not sure by whom) within three weeks. The United Nations offered assistance to refugees fleeing Israel at that time. After the family received news of Jamal's death, some family members left to go to Daraa and Damascus in Syria, others went to Deir Abu Saeed and Irbid in Jordan, and my family stayed in the Jordan Valley for approximately fifteen years. My grandfather, Mohammad, wanted the family to return to Besan, but his cousin, a man considered to be very intelligent, advised the family not to return and the family followed his counsel. My grandfather built a home in Jordan Valley and lived the remainder of his days hoping to return to Besan. He died in Jordan Valley in 1985. When the family fled Besan, my grandfather thought to grab the deed for his land in Palestine, which he gave to my father, who still has it to this day.

My father married his second cousin, and both my parents worked for a United Nations relief agency, where my father helped dispense milk, rice and other food products, and my mother taught school. After some time, my father was able to open a barbershop, and he and my mother moved to a large city, where I was born in 1966.

I was the youngest of six children. The eldest, my one and only sister, Tamara, was followed by five boys, Majid, Barhoum, Bassem, Nabil, and Muhannad. My parents were not typical as they shared household duties. My mother worked all day at school, cooked a huge midday meal, and then my father and we children would prepare and serve a light supper. All of us children were taught to help with housework, including washing floors, ironing clothes, and helping our mother with kitchen chores. My parents were blessed in that they, along with the other Palestinian refugees from 1948, were granted Jordanian citizenship. My father was quite successful as a businessman and eventually sold his barbershop to open a school and textbook supply store downtown. He was also able to build his own home.

My father's father was an imam, an Islamic religious leader. He would perform the *Athan* or call to prayer five times a day and would preach in the mosque on Fridays. He lived to between 109 and 113 years old. Because records were not accurately kept at that time, we are uncertain of his exact age. His first wife lost nine pregnancies, so he married a second wife. His second wife was my grandmother, and she provided him with five children; two girls and three boys. My father was the youngest of the sons. He lost one brother at age eighteen when he dropped dead while playing soccer. When my grandfather's first wife finally had a successful pregnancy and bore her husband a son, whom they named Nimr, which means *tiger*, my grandmother was no longer welcome in the home. She came to live with my father, who took care of his mother and his sisters until they married.

My father, Abdulrahim, was a faithful Muslim. He loved to open the mosque for morning prayers and frequently performed the *Athan*. My mother, Aisha, was a good woman and a sincere Muslim. She worked very hard, was very kind, did not talk about others, and had a servant's heart. She died at the age of sixty-three of a heart attack, brought on after surgery for colon cancer. She did not get up and walk after surgery as the doctor recommended. Pneumonia set in and she subsequently suffered a heart attack.

I lived through the civil war in Jordan in 1970. My father hid fourteen Palestinians in the water reservoir under our home. This group was loyal to Yasir Arafat and was part of the Palestinian Militia. They told my father that they needed to rest for a night before traveling to Daraa, another thirty-five kilometers beyond our city. King Hussein and the Jordanian Army were suspicious of all non-ethnic Jordanians. My father had witnessed the deaths of political Palestinians and he felt compassion for this group. They offered him 50,000 Jordanian Dinars in cash, but my father refused to take it. They urged him to take the money in case they were not successful in crossing to Syria. My father later learned that twelve men made it to Daraa and two were killed. My father was not political in any way; he simply had a kind heart. However, he put our family at great risk by hiding these men. There was much violence and our home was riddled with bullets. I remember walking outside with my father and looking at dead bodies in the street. My family fled by foot to Syria and then to Ajloun, a city in the mountains made up mostly of Christians. I was nearly four years old and was sent to Jordan Valley to stay with my aunt, my father's sister, until the violence died down.

My aunt lived with her husband and six children in one room made of mud. She either cooked outside over a wood fire or while squatting over a propane stove that sat on the floor. While the kitchen was attached to the bedroom, it could only be accessed from outdoors. The only faucet was located in the middle of the yard, and that is where dishes were washed. My aunt arranged rocks near the faucet where she set the clean dishes out to dry. The bathroom was similar to outhouses used in the United States and was made from mud as well. It was approximately one hundred feet across the yard, kitty-corner from the kitchen. She raised chickens that provided the family with fresh eggs, and made bread daily, cooked outside in a mud oven. While my aunt lived a simple life, it was a beautiful life.

When the civil war was over, I returned to my home and attended kindergarten at a Catholic school that was attached to a hospital. Because it was a private school, my parents paid an extra fee for transportation. A Volkswagen van picked me and my brother Nabil up for school each day, six days a week, Saturday through

Thursday. The drop-off point was guarded by a large statue of Mary.

I have many memories of attending that school, especially playing outside on the merry-go-round. I received six stitches in my forehead, right between my eyes, after one student spun me so fast that I fell off and hit my head. It was a blessing the school was attached to a hospital. I was simply brought to the hospital, stitched up, and sent home on the VW van with a nun escort.

On another occasion, I was sitting at the back of the classroom, which sloped downward so the teacher was in front, at the lowest point of the room. I raised my hand and asked the nun who was teaching our class if I could use the bathroom. She refused to let me go, as she believed students used the bathroom as an excuse to leave the classroom. Ten minutes later, I asked her again, and expressed that I had to go very badly. She again refused. When I was at my breaking point, I asked permission a third time. Again, she refused. As I could no longer hold it, I wet my pants while sitting quietly at my desk. After a few minutes, the nun noticed the soles of her shoes were wet and she was leaving wet footprints as she walked. She tracked where the trickle originated from, all the way to my pants. She had the honor of cleaning me up and putting me on the VW bus home, with another nun escort, as I did not have a clean change of clothes with me. From that point on, she regularly asked me and other students whether we had to use the bathroom. Thus good came out of a negative situation.

My parents sent me and Nabil to Catholic school for kindergarten and first grade only, as they wanted to provide a good foundation for our education, knowing they couldn't have us continue after that due to the expense. I believe it was my mother's insistence that we attend, as she highly valued education.

Then we followed our sister and brothers to a school sponsored by the United Nations Relief and Works Agency for Palestine Refugees in the Near East (UNRWA). We attended this school from second through ninth grade. Our school supplies were provided free of charge and we were given fish oil capsules each day. If I tried to spit them out, the teacher would give me another one and watch to ensure that I swallowed it. We also had mass vaccinations. I remember the teachers lining us up outside in the courtyard. Nurses proceeded to give us a shot in the left arm. I'm not sure if the vaccination was for smallpox or for TB. The same needle was used from student to student, although the needle was wiped with alcohol between each use. A new needle was provided after approximately ten or fifteen uses.

Because I did not like to do homework, my mom purchased a second set of workbooks that she hid at home. When I would tell her that I lost my homework or that I didn't have homework at all, she would simply pull out her set and sit down with me to make sure I completed the work.

On several occasions, when my mother was not able to catch me and make sure that I completed my homework, I escaped from the classroom by jumping out the window. During the five-minute period between classes, I would throw my bag out the window and jump after it, often landing on the bag itself. Thankfully my classroom was ground level. I would do this so I wouldn't get spanked by the teacher for not having my homework completed. The teacher would spank the back of my hand or the bottoms of my feet when I had not done my work. I was not the only student to receive this discipline. Typically four to five students a day were on the receiving end of the ruler.

After school was out, Nabil and I would go to our father's store and help him by cleaning, opening boxes of new supplies, and stocking the shelves. During vacation from school, I would set out merchandise, usually books, magazines and newspapers. I would stand in front of my father's store or on the sidewalk in a highly traveled area. My father would usually let me keep twenty to twenty-five percent of the sales. I saved this money and used it to purchase toy guns, fireworks, and eventually a bike.

Because my father was successful in business, I believe that my siblings were spoiled. My father provided us with anything we desired materially while there were extended members of our family who greatly struggled financially. I believe my father was motivated by simply wanting to bless his children as he was blessed. He was able to buy several vehicles, one of them new. I remember unwrapping the factory plastic off the 1980 626 Mazda he purchased. We boys loved cars and were wild drivers.

My only sister, Tamara, is married to an ethnic Jordanian and they have four children. They live in a suburb of Amman, the capital of Jordan. Her husband owns a school supply store. He was formerly with the Merchant Marines and he speaks English quite well. He also has a wonderful sense of humor and loves to laugh. A running joke in their family is that, when he asks his children if they are Jordanian or Palestinian, they say, "We are Jordanian!" and if the Palestinian side of the family asks them the same question, they say, "We are Palestinian!" While Jordan has come a long way in absorbing and acknowledging the Palestinians, especially since both King Hussein and his son Abdullah married Palestinian women, there are still underlying tensions between ethnic Jordanians and Palestinians. For example, the best government positions go to Jordanians.

My eldest brother, Majid, suffered from stuttering as a child and was made fun of terribly, including by our family. He eventually outgrew his stuttering and obtained a college degree in accounting. He worked on and off for our father and younger brother in the bookshop. He also spent a short time working in the

United Arab Emirates. His wife works in the Jordanian Police Department, while he takes care of their four children at home.

My second brother, Barhoum, always loved the West. He was very smart but did not like to study. At age sixteen, he was able to study in Oxford, England for a year. He loved it and, after that experience, purposed to study abroad again. He dreamed of going to America and, after his younger brother, Bassem, traveled to the United States to study, he followed. He eventually did make it to the United States and he studied there on and off for three years before ultimately getting deported due to being out of status. I will write more about his story shortly.

My third brother, Bassem, dreamed of studying in the United States. He traveled to Texas, where he studied English and took the Test Of English as a Foreign Language (TOEFL) exam, which was required for entrance into an American university. He then studied in the Midwest and obtained his engineering degree. He and his American wife and son have lived throughout the U.S.

My fourth brother, Nabil, is a hard worker. He is one year older than me and we were often thought to be twins. We were very close growing up. He studied at Yarmouk University and obtained a degree in journalism. Ultimately, however, his love was business, and he took over running our father's store. I was his assistant. He moved to the U.S. in 2002. He was granted asylum, and his wife and four children joined him in the U.S. in 2008. He runs two successful businesses, a smoke shop and a grocery store, and is considering opening a third, a pizza franchise.

My father used to say that he didn't have real estate, but he had five boys, and each of us was equal to five big buildings. He meant that he didn't invest in land, he invested in us. Looking back, I realize that he did not include my sister in this saying. However, he was very loving to all of us, including my sister.

Because my parents put all my brothers through college, except for me, they put their vehicle titles in my name at my mother's request. Because my family lost a lot of money and began struggling after sending their two sons to America to study, we began to suffer financially. My father bought a van, and my job was to travel all around Jordan to the small cities and villages and sell school supplies. I did not like being confined, so I loved my traveling job. I made good sales and would bring Nabil all the money at the end of each day. I was able to keep a small amount to buy food, tea, hummus, and cigarettes, as I was a heavy smoker.

Jordan has a mandatory two-year military obligation for men starting at age eighteen. Exceptions are available if one is the only son, attends college, has a medical issue, or works in a position that is irreplaceable by another individual. My father was able to pay officials and keep all of my brothers out of the service except for me and my eldest brother, Majid. Majid was given a daytime desk job and did not have to stay at the barracks. I always wanted to be in the military and did not ask my father for help to get out of it. I was assigned to the military police, and completed my military service in 1986.

I remember a time when I was serving near Hama (close to Syria and Israel). I was looking across the Jordan River at an Israeli soldier. The soldier pointed his gun at me and I fled. I also remember getting lost in the desert when our radio communications got disconnected. I survived for three days on four pieces of pita bread and some olives my mother had packed for me. I witnessed a new trainee getting so frightened during hand grenade training that he blew himself up and died.

I was always a free spirit and considered very wild. Once, in an attempt to be like my father, I convinced a neighbor boy to sit quietly so I could give him a haircut. The boy was two years younger than me and scared, so he complied. I gave him a very bad hair cut that could only be repaired by shaving his head. I also cut aerial TV antennas on my home and on homes throughout the neighborhood, causing them to be without TV for a night or two. My father gave me several toy cars, which I smashed in an effort to find out what was inside them and how they were made. On another occasion, I hid under the sofa and lit matches, eventually setting the sofa on fire. However, people always loved me and I was shown great favor by people in power, such as decorated military officers, police chiefs, judges, the Jordanian Security Services (similar to the FBI), and government officials in charge of passports and the postal service. I met many of these people when I sold school supplies out of my van.

I also had an affinity for friendship with Christians. Most of my friendships were with Christians, growing up. We had Armenian neighbors and I also had a number of Catholic friends, including Jordanian Christians.

My good friend, Jamal, and I loved to hunt, and would often hunt pheasants and pigeons near Ajloun and on the hillside in Jordan Valley. We would find pheasants in orange groves owned by private farmers and the farmers would permit us to hunt there. We would hunt and then cook the birds over a fire and make tea. We also decided we would look for treasure (a common pastime, due to the many conquerors in Jordan's past). One night, Jamal and I went to a Turkish cemetery at 3:00 in the morning. Most of the graves were in the ground, but there were also caves in the cemetery. Jamal and I opened one of the caves by removing large black stones blocking the entrance. I entered the cave feet first. When my head was still above ground, a woman dressed in black came to me and offered me tea. The woman was standing on the ground outside the cave, about three to four feet from my head. I jumped out and ran to the van. Jamal witnessed the woman talking to me, saw her disappear, and followed me, running to the van. We took off like crazy because we knew that the woman was some kind of evil spirit, and we were happy to get away alive. We left our shovels and equipment at the cemetery, and I was sick for two weeks with the chills, fever, and shaking.

The brother closest to me in age, Nabil, had his eye on our second cousin, Nora, as a future wife. He was set on her for years. He asked my father to go with him to request her hand in marriage. My father took me with him as well. My uncle said that he would give my brother consent to marry Nora, but he asked that I, the younger brother, would marry her older sister, Alia. I knew that my brother had his heart set on our cousin, so out of respect for my father and not really thinking much about it, I said that yes, I would marry the older sister. That night, I couldn't sleep. I tossed and turned, thinking, "What have I gotten myself into?!" The next day, my uncle came to visit me and my father. His eldest daughter had confessed that she was in love with her first cousin on her mother's side. She wanted to marry him, not me. My uncle swore that he would step on her head and force her to marry me. I thought, "Why would I want to marry someone who doesn't want me?" I told my uncle so and released him and his eldest daughter from their engagement obligations. My father's pride was hurt and he carried on for a while, but I was so relieved! And my brother Nabil was so happy. It was a win-win for everyone.

My second-eldest brother, Barhoum, studied English in Ohio, where his Palestinian girlfriend was also attending school. They both returned to Jordan, broke up, and when our brother Bassem left Texas and went to Iowa to study, Barhoum followed him there. Bassem studied at a state university, and Barhoum began his studies at a good Lutheran college.

Growing Up Muslim

I was circumcised when I was three years old. I remember the person certified to perform the circumcision, Mr. Shalaby, arriving at our home. I was so excited as my parents and siblings dressed me in special clothing and told me it would be fun to celebrate after it was over. My mom told me, "After this, you will be a good looking man." I had been anxiously waiting Mr. Shalaby's arrival, holding on to the railing of our front porch. I saw him get out of the car, holding a black briefcase. I jumped up and down saying, "He is here! He is here!" My mom had me prepped. I was wearing a white dish dasha with white, long pants underneath. Mr. Shalaby shook my hand and asked me if I was ready. I said "yes," not realizing how painful the experience would be. My parents had removed the sofa from the living room and had moved a single bed there in its place. I was told to lie down. My father stood over my head, held my hands, and said, "It's going to be okay, son." My brother, Majid, stood on the other side of my head, and my brother Barhoum stood at my feet and held them down. My mom, sister and aunts waited in another room. Mr. Shalaby told me it would take approximately ten minutes. It was the longest ten minutes of my childhood. He opened his briefcase, which featured a formidable display of many sharp tools and gold-plated blades. My father told me not to look. The second I felt it, I started to scream non-stop and cry. Mr. Shalaby wrapped me in cotton and left. I didn't move or leave my bed for three hours. I was given something for pain and brought a plate of desserts: halawa, harisa, kinafa, and toffee. I was in pain for two days. My mother doted on me, gave me toy cars, and fed me whatever I asked for. It took me a week to fully recover.

I remember going to the mosque with my father one to two times a day. My father also took me with him to the open market every morning to buy fruits and vegetables, as these items were purchased fresh each day.

I remember my grandfather coming to visit my father's store. He would stand outside in his abaya and yell, "Abdulrahim" in a deep voice. Then my father would respond, "Welcome, father!" My father would bring a chair for him to sit outside, as my grandfather did not like to sit in the store because it was too small and cramped.

My grandfather told me a story that I've never forgotten. One day a grandfather and grandson were journeying across the desert on a camel. At the first town they arrived at, the townspeople told them that the desert was too hot and they were showing no mercy to the camel by both riding it. After hearing these comments, the grandfather got off and only the grandson rode the camel. At the second town, the townspeople commented that the grandson had no respect by allowing his grandfather to walk while he rode the camel. So the grandson got off and walked while the grandfather rode the camel. At the third town, the townspeople commented that the grandfather had no mercy for his grandson because he allowed a little child to walk while he rode. Then both the grandfather and grandson walked by the side of the camel. At the fourth town, the townspeople commented on how foolish the grandfather and grandson were to walk when they had a perfectly good camel to ride on. My grandfather told me that I should make my own decisions in life. He told me to stick with my decision because, no matter what decision I would make, people would find something to comment on and disagree with. Essentially, it is impossible to make everyone happy, so make decisions based on what your heart tells you and don't second guess yourself based on people's opinions.

Throughout my growing up years, we received many visitors. It was typical to have company five days a week or more. As dictated by Arab hospitality and tradition, unspoken rules define the hospitality process. When visitors arrive, they are served tea and whatever is available at the moment, such as fruit. After visiting for some time, my mom and sister would serve some mixed nuts or ice cream. Then, an hour or so later, when the visitors would express the need to leave, my mom would prepare and serve Arabic coffee. After drinking the coffee, guests would depart.

The most fun I experienced as a child was during Ramadan and the two Eid holidays. The first Eid takes place after Ramadan, the month of fasting. The second Eid takes place seventy days later, during the time of Haj to Mecca.

During Ramadan, we fast from the time of the first prayer, around 4:00 a.m. (approximately an hour-and-a-half before sunrise) to sunset. Ramadan typically lasts between twenty-nine and thirty-one days, beginning when the New Moon is sighted. Ramadan was painful due to the inability to eat or drink all day, especially when it took place during the long days of summer. I used to have a lot of fun helping my family prepare the meal to break the fast, as well as setting the table. During this month, we would often invite relatives and friends over to eat. We were also invited to their homes. After eating, we would sit down in the living room, drink tea and coffee, eat dessert, and watch special programming aired during Ramadan, such as comedies or historical series. Sometimes my parents would have guests over and sometimes they would go out and visit relatives.

During Ramadan, there are special Tarawih prayers held nightly at the mosque. My father would go to the mosque to pray and my brothers and I would go downtown and open my father's store. We would buy sweets from the bakery, sometimes eating at the bakery, and other times bringing the sweets back to the store to eat with our friends. During the last week of Ramadan, downtown is packed, similar to Times Square on New Year's Eve. People go there to shop and buy new clothing for Eid. When the New Moon is sighted, this marks the last day of Ramadan and the beginning of three-day Eid al Fitr which means *Feast of Breaking the Fast.*

My parents taught us that the purpose of Ramadan was to learn sacrifice, self-control, discipline, and empathy for people less fortunate than us. This was also a time to show generosity. For example, my father would provide a meal for another family each day of Ramadan. We were also taught the importance of spending extra time reading the Quran, praying, asking God to forgive us, and striving to be obedient.

The night before Eid, the whole city is awake. Barber shops, retailers and restaurants are open until 5:00 a.m. The only businesses that are not open are banks, and hardware and furniture stores. My parents would not typically buy new clothing or shoes for themselves at this time, but they would make sure my sister and brothers had new clothing and money. When we were little, we would receive about two dinars, approximately five U.S. dollars. As we grew, we were given more money, up to twenty dinars, or approximately fifty U.S. dollars. My father would typically give my sister more money individually than he would give each of us boys.

The next day, the first day of Eid, my entire family would travel to the cemetery to visit the graves of deceased relatives. We would make sure to get there by sunrise. My parents taught us that the dead could hear and see those visiting on this day. We would then return home to eat breakfast. Eid breakfast was lamb kidneys and liver, hummus, falafel, ful, bread and tea.

After breakfast, I would go with my father and brothers to visit his brothers and sisters. Meanwhile, my mother and sister would stay at home, waiting for my mother's brothers and sister to visit at our house. The second day of Eid, I would go with my father and brothers to visit second and third cousins and other relatives. My mother and sister stayed at the house throughout Eid to serve all the people who would come to visit. Eid visits typically last ten to fifteen minutes and involve the giving of money to sisters, nieces and nephews. Adult men do not give money to other adult males, only to their adult sisters or their mother. Because there are so many relatives and friends to visit during Eid, and to allow the process to go faster, guests are served coffee, sweets and candy. My Christian friends would come to my home to wish me a happy Eid as well.

When I was little, we would go to Jordan Valley and visit my grandfather and my father's sister. As I got older, my brothers and I would go on rides, rent bicycles, and would come home with rips in our brand new clothes due to the cuffs of our pants rubbing against the bike chains. We also loved to buy fireworks and set them off in the middle of the street after dark. Sometimes the neighborhood kids would make a bonfire in an empty lot and talk, arriving home after midnight smelling like smoke, dirty and tired.

The second Eid is Eid al-Adha or *Feast of the Sacrifice.* During this four-day holiday, Muslims remember Abraham's willingness to sacrifice Ishmael. This is also the time of Haj or pilgrimage to Mecca. Haj is one of the five pillars of Islam. Every Muslim is required to go to Mecca and perform Haj if they have the finances to do so. Islam mandates that seven sheep are to be sacrificed for each person during his or her lifetime. The meat is divided into three parts. One third is kept for one's family, one third is given to family, friends and neighbors, and one third is given to the needy. This is another way to connect with God, promote one's entrance into heaven, exhibit obedience, and hopefully obtain forgiveness. My father would usually sacrifice two or three sheep at this time, however many he could afford. My father would give me and my brothers the meat and we would deliver it to those it was intended for.

While people are at Haj, their family will decorate the inside and outside of the home with pine or olive branches and lights. It is particularly important to decorate the front entrance. My parents were both able to make Haj. Upon returning from Haj, men are called *Haj* and women are called *Haji,* to show respect.

Every Friday, my brothers and I went with my father to the mosque for Jummah prayer. We were required to do so by my parents. I usually liked the speech given by the imam before the prayer and I enjoyed these times with my father and brothers. After praying, we would stop at the market and buy fruit to bring home.

My mom and sister would have the meal ready. It was

the biggest meal of the week and usually included lots

of lamb or chicken.

Carrie's Background

A round the same time that Barhoum attended the Lutheran college, an American girl named Carrie graduated high school a semester early and began attending the same college. Raised by conservative Christian parents, David and Shirley, she had always had a love for the Middle East. She grew up listening to her father read out of the Old Testament after family dinners. Her great-grandfather on her paternal grandmother's side was an officer in the Salvation Army. Her paternal grandmother traveled with an evangelist as his organist.

Carrie's grandfather's father, Albert, had married later in life. Carrie was named after his wife, her great-grandmother. He purchased land throughout the United States and ultimately settled his wife and

seven children in California. His eldest daughter graduated from Stanford University in bacteriology and
was extremely intelligent. She married a man from
the Middle East, which was relatively unheard of at
that time. Carrie highly respected this great-aunt and
admired her very much. When the eldest son had completed one year at Stanford with the goal of studying
law, his father told him and his younger brother, Robert
(Carrie's grandfather), that they were to move to another
state where he had land and run the farm. Robert, too,
had yearned to go to college. He was never able to
do so, but he never lost his love for learning. While he
farmed all his life, he had an office in the basement
of his home stacked with academic books in subjects
such as chemistry and engineering, and he would read
them when he had time.

Robert was a quiet, hard-working man who did not
like any attention on himself. He could be considered
a workaholic, yet he never farmed on Sunday. He
faithfully read his Bible and loved the Lord. His wife
loved music, played piano, and was organist at the
Methodist church they attended. They were blessed
with eight children and had a very busy home. His wife

was diagnosed with cancer in her early forties and died when their youngest daughter was only eight years old.

After many years as a single father, Robert fell in love with a Norwegian Lutheran, Erma, on the other side of the river. Erma had six children and had lost her husband to kidney disease when he was very young. They married the same year Carrie was born, and Erma brought her three youngest boys to live on the farm. Erma was and is known for excellent cooking and baking, has a reputation as the best bun baker in the entire area, and simply loves everyone. Carrie has never known her to ever speak ill of anyone. Anyone and everyone who comes to her home is welcomed, fed and loved. While Robert died in 1991, Erma has continued an active and vital role in his children's, grandchildren's and great-grandchildren's lives, and she has been an example of Christ's love throughout Carrie's life.

All eight children in Carrie's grandfather's family served the Lord in various capacities.

David's eldest brother was a graduate of Moody Bible Institute and a pilot with Mission Aviation Fellowship. He was delivering supplies to other missionaries in a jungle in the Philippines in preparation for Christmas when his plane crashed, and both he and the pastor with him were killed. He left behind his pregnant wife and three children. His wife never remarried and is a missionary to this day, having served in China, Greece, and other countries. All four of her children are missionaries: two sons are pilots, one daughter married a man from Greece and lives there, and her youngest daughter has served in Greece as well.

David's eldest sister and her husband were missionaries to the Middle East and later to the Philippines. His second sister's husband worked as an accountant for the Billy Graham Evangelistic Association (BGEA) and would drive the Reverend Billy Graham from the airport to the hotel to BGEA headquarters when he would visit. His third sister and her husband have served in China, and his youngest sister and husband were missionaries to Nepal. David's two younger brothers are sincere Christians and raised their families to love the Lord. So Carrie had a strong Christian heritage.

While growing up, the missionary relatives would come home to the United States on furlough every four years. She had many memories of sitting in her great-uncle's home where all the extended family was gathered, and watching slides of natives in other countries projected on the wall. She knew then, at a very young age, that she wanted to be a missionary as well.

David received an agricultural engineering degree. Because he was told by his father since he was a young boy that he was to work on the family farm, he immediately moved to the farm upon graduating college. Carrie's mother, Shirley, had a social work degree and worked as a social worker until Carrie was born. At that time, she gave up her job to be a full-time stay-at-home wife and mother.

Carrie was the eldest of two children, with a brother two years younger than her. She was a typical eldest child, trying to please others by performing well. She was a top student, played sports (although she was not very skilled), participated in 4-H, and was church organist. Many Sunday mornings, she would travel to the three churches belonging to her Lutheran parish. She received her first speeding ticket while attempting to keep up with the minister who had left for the next church before she completed the final hymn. When she arrived late to the next church and explained that she had received a speeding ticket and why, the minister was not too happy with her.

Carrie always loved Israel. In sixth grade, her class was given a drawing assignment. She immediately went to the encyclopedia, looked up Israel, and found a picture of the Dome of the Rock mosque, which she drew for her project. Her nickname as a basketball player was *Rabbi* because everyone in her small high school knew she dreamed of living in Israel.

When her parents married, her father was Methodist and her mother was Lutheran. They met at a Christian Intervarsity meeting. After marrying, they attended the Assembly of God church until Carrie was about age seven or eight. After this, her parents attended a Lutheran church, where Carrie was confirmed. Her parents were always seeking the Lord and ended up getting involved in the Charismatic Movement of the 1980s. They would drive near and far, to coffee houses and gyms and Bible camps to hear people speak.

One summer when Carrie was eleven, her parents attended Hungry Horse Bible Camp to hear Pastor William Mjorud. It was there that she received the gift of the Holy Spirit. That same year, Carrie's mother became friends with a local woman, Agnes. It quickly became apparent that this woman had a close relationship with Christ, and Carrie grew up under the godly wisdom and direction she provided. When she was approximately age fourteen, another Christian friend, Videll, who operated in the prophetic gifts, told Carrie that she and her husband would be laborers in the end-time harvest and that they would have three blonde daughters.

Videll, in turn, introduced Carrie and her parents to a woman named Betty, who was an Endtime Handmaiden of the Lord, part of the ministry of Sister Gwen Shaw. Sister Gwen passed away January 2013. Carrie was fascinated with Sister Gwen's ministry to communist countries and read many books by her. Carrie's senior year of high school, in October 1986, her parents gave her the opportunity of a lifetime – the chance to travel to Israel with the Endtime Handmaidens. It was a ten-day trip and took place during the Feast of Tabernacles.

This trip was the highlight of Carrie's life. The second she landed on Israeli soil, she felt she had arrived home. Sister Gwen's group visited throughout Israel, spent time praying in the Upper Room, went to Qumran, and traveled on foot with people from the

Christian Embassy and other Christians throughout Jerusalem. They also participated in Feast of Tabernacles events, heard Shimon Perez speak, and then were able to shake his hand afterwards. Carrie didn't want the trip to end.

The trip to Israel changed Carrie forever. Her heart was burning to return, and real life paled in comparison. She located a synagogue near her small home town and began attending Shabbat services. She remained in touch with the Endtime Handmaidens for two or three more years and attended one convention in St. Louis, but after that had no more connection with the ministry as she felt she had failed in her Christian walk and was not committed or worthy enough of Endtime Handmaiden caliber.

Her mother petitioned the school superintendent to allow Carrie to leave high school after the completion of her first semester in December. The superintendent agreed and Carrie entered the Lutheran College where Barhoum was studying, in January 1987, at the age of seventeen.

Carrie's parents thought it would be a good, safe school for their somewhat sheltered daughter to begin college. The son of a former Lutheran pastor and their friends' children also attended the college. Interestingly, her first day on campus, while walking into the administrative offices, she met a man named Barhoum. Because his TOEFL grade was low, as well as his high school and Jordanian university scores, only a private school would admit him. In comparison, his brother Bassem's scores were higher so Bassem was accepted into a state university.

Even more interesting, this same man was in her African History class. He soon began holding the door open for her and asked her where she was from. She was wearing a gold Star of David necklace, a keepsake from her trip to Israel. Barhoum kept asking her out for coffee and she kept refusing because she said her parents didn't allow her to date.

Eventually Barhoum wore her down and they went out for coffee. She learned then he was a Palestinian Jordanian, studying in the U.S. with his brother, Bassem. He was intense like no other person Carrie had ever met. He loved people, was passionate about life, would not eat all day, smoking like a chimney, and then would cook a huge feast at night and eat an entire chicken himself around 1 or 2 a.m. Everything he set his hand to was done with great enthusiasm and passion and he oozed self-esteem, something that Carrie lacked.

Carrie typically traveled home to the farm every weekend. After beginning to date Barhoum, she would go to the farm for the weekend and then become anxious if she didn't get back to campus on time. This was because Barhoum would get angry with her if she ran late. He would insist on spending every waking minute together, and would monitor who she talked to and when. As Barhoum's friends would tell Carrie, "Barhoum is crazy about you. He loves you like no one else will love you in your life. We've never seen anyone love someone like he loves you." But this love came at a price of control and jealousy. Carrie's parents became alarmed by Barhoum's hold on their daughter.

Barhoum first asked Carrie to marry him on St. Patrick's Day 1987, less than two months after meeting her. He continued to pressure her about marriage. She went home in May 1987 to participate in her high school graduation ceremony. Barhoum attended the ceremony and spent the remainder of the day and evening at her party on the farm. He gave her an engraved watch with a small diamond as a graduation gift.

At the graduation party, Carrie's family friend, Agnes, talked with Barhoum at great length and told him that he must leave Carrie alone. Agnes told him, "Do not touch God's anointed." Carrie felt pulled between Barhoum and her parents, and all her dreams of becoming a missionary seemed to be going up in smoke.

During the summer, Barhoum was allowed to visit her several times. He wrote her many long letters, and he was allowed to call. However, he would call in the middle of the night and would keep Carrie on the phone longer than she was allowed. There was continual tension and fighting between Carrie and her parents (as Carrie defended Barhoum to them) and Carrie and Barhoum (as Carrie defended her parents to Barhoum). In mid-July, Barhoum came to visit her without permission and told her to pack up and move out of her parents' home. Carrie just wanted peace and there was none to be found. She left with Barhoum on this hot, humid July evening, and the drive to her college town is engraved on her memory forever. After spending three weeks with Barhoum, her parents suggested counseling for her, Barhoum, and the family, and she returned to the farm. Surprisingly, her parents allowed her to return to school the fall of 1987. Because of the efforts of all the parties involved to improve communication, and Carrie's agreement at her parents' urging to get involved on campus and meet more young people, she enrolled in another school term. Despite sincere intentions to participate more fully in campus life, Carrie was very shy, had a hard time socializing, and thus attended classes sporadically and spent more and more time with Barhoum and his friends.

In December 1987, nearly one year after meeting Barhoum, Carrie became pregnant. Barhoum was convinced that this was the only way to win her parents' support and approval for their marriage. When Carrie first began attending college, she was surprised at the level of promiscuity on the part of the students, even those who traveled to perform musically at churches on weekends. She felt that many students were not interested in faith at all. And she was further disappointed when she realized that many of the professors were not teaching Christianity. She quickly became disillusioned with the hypocrisy she witnessed on campus.

At the same time, Barhoum did not want her spending any time with her roommate and, as she met him her first day of school, she had not made any friends on her own. So Barhoum, his brother, his brother's girlfriend, and the typical American groupies that often surround international students, became Carrie's social culture and identity. She witnessed the parties and was surrounded by young people living together. Over a short period of time, she was living this same lifestyle. At one point Bassem's girlfriend, a good Catholic girl, warned Carrie not to sleep with Barhoum. She told Carrie that she had made the mistake of not waiting for marriage and how she deeply regretted it. Carrie appreciated this woman's advice, but it was already too late.

While Carrie accepts full responsibility for her actions, she lived a controlled and sheltered life under her parents, and was then culture shocked by what she encountered in the real world. She felt that she had not been educated or equipped in any way to deal with what she met at college. Further, because Barhoum was nearly nine years older than her, and extremely persistent and controlling, she felt she didn't have a voice. She felt she had never developed the ability to think on her own. She felt unable to identify what she truly believed anymore; she was very confused and conflicted. When Carrie first met Barhoum, she was very clear about her faith and her dreams of being a missionary. She also felt that she would be able to witness to Barhoum and lead him to Christ. While Barhoum had a very kind heart, was generous, and loved to help others, he was surrounded by Muslim friends who were living it up and Carrie, too, became immersed in that lifestyle. The world was not nearly as black and white as she had thought and she was trying to take it all in while simultaneously processing it.

The first intifada took place in December 1987 and there was a lot of political commentary at the time. There were many on campus sympathetic to the Palestinian cause, and Barhoum was interviewed and appeared on a local news channel discussing the situation. While Carrie had always been a staunch supporter of Israel, she now began to re-examine the situation, and tried to see it through Palestinian eyes instead of only through an Israeli lens. However, her heart would always go back to the Bible and what God had said about the land of Israel. She did, however, begin to develop a concern and care for the Palestinians that she had never experienced, as she had never attempted to learn about them prior to Barhoum's influence on her life.

Barhoum participated in Toastmasters and would take Carrie with him. He loved public speaking. He also loved to write and would often write poems. He was adamant about how much he loved Carrie and about how he could not live without her. She tried to break up with him on several occasions, but he would become distraught and even threatened to kill himself – one time pulling out a knife and holding it to his throat.

Carrie finally consented to marry Barhoum, and the ceremony was to be performed by a Methodist pastor in a nearby town. Carrie's parents, her brother, and Barhoum's brother, Bassem, attended. Barhoum said, "I do" and when it was Carrie's turn, she said she had to go to the restroom to think. She never came out and they were not married. It wasn't that she didn't deeply care about Barhoum, she just didn't know who she was anymore and she needed time and space to think and sort things out. Underlying it all, she wanted to be obedient to God's best, and she knew that marrying a non-Christian was not God's best.

Throughout the relationship, Carrie would discuss Christ with Barhoum. She would tell him that she could not marry a non-Christian. Barhoum would attend church with her on occasion and he had agreed to attend Christian counseling with Carrie when her parents suggested it. Ironically, the Christian counselor was totally taken in by Barhoum's charm, and the counseling was not very effective in that it did not resolve any issues, but, in a sense, created more. Carrie felt that more effort was put on helping Barhoum and his feelings of being kept on the outside by her parents, rather than helping her sort through her feelings to help her develop the strength to stand up for herself.

Barhoum attended services with Carrie at an Assembly of God church, at her local Lutheran church, and then also attended a non-denominational church near Carrie's hometown. Carrie and Barhoum attended pre-marriage counseling at her Lutheran church. The pastor was very kind and kept wringing his hands and explaining how very, very difficult marriage was in the best of circumstances. He repeated this many times, and both Carrie and Barhoum left wondering how marriage could really be as full of trials as this pastor suggested. Ironically, the pastor and his wife later divorced, so the pastor was likely sharing from his heart about his personal experience with the difficulties of marriage.

The pastor of the non-denominational church near her hometown was a former military man, married to a woman from abroad, and familiar with the Endtime Handmaidens ministry. This pastor and his wife took to Barhoum immediately and were very protective of him. In particular, they seemed to support Barhoum's idea that Carrie's parents did not approve of him because of discriminatory reasons, rather than the fact that Barhoum was of a different faith and had tendencies to be controlling. This couple often invited Barhoum to stay with them on weekends, and the pastor took Barhoum with him to an evangelism conference in another state. Upon his return from this conference, Barhoum told Carrie that he had accepted Christ. However, Carrie never knew if it was from the heart or whether it was to appease her. She sincerely hoped that he had made a heart decision, but she didn't necessarily see fruit in that regard.

In September 1988, Barhoum and Carrie's daughter, Änna, was born. Carrie's parents had taken her to a Christian pregnancy center where she received periodic counseling. Barhoum attended at times as well. The counselor encouraged adoption and Carrie's parents were also supportive of this. Carrie prayed about it and seriously considered adoption. Barhoum was never supportive of adoption and did not want Carrie to speak of it. At one point, Carrie asked the counselor, who had three boys and had always wanted a girl, if she would consider adopting her child. The counselor said that she was honored to be asked, but that she could not adopt Carrie's baby. After seeing and holding her baby, Carrie knew adoption was not an option. Her parents told her that if she would break up with Barhoum, they would take her and Änna home to live with them and they would make sure that Carrie received her college education. She accepted this offer. The counselor attended Änna's subsequent baptism at Carrie's hometown Lutheran church and served as Änna's sponsor.

In January 1989, Carrie's parents moved her and Änna to a large city, where Carrie enrolled at a private university. Carrie's great-grandmother, also named Carrie, had attended this university when it was a Methodist teacher's college, so it seemed a good school choice. The first day Carrie visited campus, she noticed that there was an Israeli professor who led archeological trips to Israel. She signed up for every one of his classes. She majored in International Studies with a focus on the Middle East, and minored in Jewish Studies.

Carrie loved studying at the university. It was an amazing school where students were basically kind to one another and many of them had a heart for the nations. Carrie was a member of the Political Science Club and she participated in a mock United Nations. While she always wanted to go on one of her professor's archeological trips, she was never able to come up with the funds to do so.

Carrie kept in touch with Barhoum via telephone and he would often write to her. He ended up attending school at a state university in Wisconsin, and came to visit Carrie and Änna. Eventually he was arrested while taking an exam because he had fallen out of status. Because of the drama and emotional stress of his relationship with Carrie and her parents' disapproval, followed by her pregnancy and the birth of their child, he had not attended class full-time as mandated by his student visa. Thus he violated the terms of his visa, requiring him to leave the United States. Carrie later learned that the police officer in her home town had assisted in alerting authorities to Barhoum being out of status. This same officer told Shirley that he had done so because he believed Carrie was a good girl and he was concerned for her safety. While Barhoum waited for deportation, Carrie went to visit him in a Wisconsin county jail. She held Änna up to the little window in the door of the jail so Barhoum could see his daughter. Soon after, in July 1989, he was deported back to Jordan. I picked him up from the airport in Amman and drove him home.

Carrie kept in touch with my family, sending photos of Änna and writing letters. In turn, they too sent cards and greetings through my brother Bassem who was attending school in Iowa. Bassem would visit Carrie and Änna regularly and was a good uncle to Änna.

Barhoum and Carrie wrote to one another and talked on the phone. He eventually went to the United

Arab Emirates (UAE), where he worked as an insurance claims investigator and made good money. He sent as much money home as possible to assist our parents. He would send gifts and money to Carrie and Änna as well.

Barhoum was loyal to his family and to his parents above all else. He loved his family and his friends with a fierce, intense loyalty, and would go to great lengths to help anyone in trouble, even when it put him in jeopardy financially or otherwise. While Carrie loved Barhoum, she felt that his influence on her life did not bring out the best in her. She prayed and prayed and struggled and struggled. She had been raised to think that, in most situations, children should be raised by both parents. She watched Änna growing up, saw Änna's similarities to her father, and agonized as to what was best. Barhoum was adamant that Carrie and Änna should join him in the Emirates upon Carrie's graduation from college. As Barhoum had a ten-year bar from reentering the United States, the only way to be reunited as a family would be for Carrie and Änna to move to the Middle East. Carrie could not imagine her life without Barhoum. He had such an intense presence, he was larger than life, and she felt that ultimately she would not be able to continue her life without him because she felt his hold on her, even though he was across the world. He professed that he was now a Christian and he wrote beautiful letters to Carrie and Änna, encouraging them to read the Bible and serve Christ.

Barhoum wrote to Carrie regularly and she would receive her mail at the student post office. One day she opened a letter from Barhoum, telling her about a dream he had had. In this dream, he and I were standing together in an area where we lived in Jordan, and Carrie approached us, expressing her anger and frustration at Barhoum for leaving her alone. In the dream, I told Barhoum, "She is right, Barhoum, and you have no right doing this to Carrie." Barhoum described the dream to Carrie in great detail, including what she was wearing.

Carrie knew who I (Muhannad) was, because when she was dating Barhoum, she spent a lot of time at the house he shared with Bassem. They would talk about their family at great length and would describe their youngest brother Muhannad as the tallest and kindest brother of the family. At this time, they were trying to convince me and my father to travel to the United States. I was interested in attending a mechanic school in Russia and had no desire to come to the U.S. Then my father had a painful episode with a slipped disk in his back, and travel was out of the question for him. Thus the talk of bringing family to the U.S. was dropped.

At one time, while talking on the phone, Barhoum shared that he was having health problems and that there was something wrong with his blood. He said he was going in for more tests. Carrie did not take him too seriously, because he had gone through many health scares and he could be quite dramatic. She thought it was possibly for attention rather than a serious concern.

In May 1991, several weeks after Barhoum had expressed his health concerns, Carrie was talking to him on the phone. He was very excited and was telling her how he was going to confront a Saudi company doing business in the UAE about the fact that it had set fire to its buildings to collect the insurance money. Carrie cautioned him to be careful and to not be confrontational. Änna got on the phone and sang her *ABCs* to her father.

The following Sunday, Carrie was studying for final exams. Our brother, Bassem, and his wife took Änna to the zoo so Carrie could study. In the middle of studying, she suddenly felt Barhoum's presence in the room. She looked up, expecting to see him there, because he always told her, "When you least expect it, I'll be with you. I will always be there for you." She could not see him, but she knew he was there.

Later that evening, she tried calling him to tell him of this experience. He did not answer his phone. She called his company, and the company secretary said he was not at work. She called his family in Jordan, but the phone was busy for hours and she could not get through.

On Monday, Bassem called Carrie to tell her that Barhoum had died. His body was found under a tree on the side of a busy UAE highway. He had pulled his car over, gotten out, and died.

The government would not allow any family members into the country to get the body or to collect any personal effects. The coroner's report said that Barhoum had died of a heart attack. However, Carrie suspected that he had been deliberately poisoned or killed by the people he went to confront. We will never know the true story of how he really died.

Carrie spent many hours in her apartment, surrounded by Barhoum's letters, crying and asking God "Why?" She had lost her beloved grandfather, Robert, in January that year after his extremely painful battle with bone cancer, and this second loss was very difficult. The middle of the night was the hardest. She would be unable to sleep and she would pour her heart out to God. She would also talk to Barhoum and tell him all the things she had been unable to tell him while he was alive.

Months later, Bassem went to visit Carrie at her apartment. He said that his mother had a proposal, and he asked if Carrie wanted to hear it. Carrie said yes, and he shared that his mother would be pleased if Carrie would marry her youngest son, Muhannad (me), and keep Änna in the family. I had already agreed to this and the final decision rested with Carrie. My parents were supportive of me marrying Carrie as Islam allows Muslim men to marry Christian women. My mother would never have asked me to marry Carrie if she thought it was against Islam. Further, my mother was making a great sacrifice as she knew, if I married Carrie, I would likely leave Jordan and live in the United States.

Carrie had tried dating as a single mother. It did not go well. She hated the small talk and trying to be someone she was not. She attended church at Living Word. She attempted to go to some single Christian gatherings, but she was lonely and discouraged, and still mourning the loss of Barhoum.

Carrie remembered the dream Barhoum had about me. She remembered all the good things my brothers had to say about me. She thought, "Who could love my daughter more than her uncle?" And so Carrie agreed to marry me.

It is not uncommon in the Middle East for a man to marry his brother's widow. There are examples of this in the Bible. Further, I had a real life example in my family. A first cousin of mine, Tarek, was a veterinarian. He married and had five children. He struggled with kidney disease and eventually died. After his death, his younger brother, Hatem, married Tarek's widow. Hatem was a medical doctor. He and his wife went on to have five children of their own. Hatem is beloved by our entire family and beloved by his brother's children, as well as his own children. He provided for all ten children, put them all through university, and they are all successful professionals. Hatem is the doctor who diagnosed my mother with cancer. All the family relies on his medical expertise, and he is known for his kindness.

We talked by phone for months (Carrie eventually had to sell the piano her parents had given her to pay her phone bill), and my cousin, an English major, would translate our letters to one another. I mailed Carrie a gold ring. When she opened the envelope while sitting in her car, the ring fell out and she could not locate it. I promptly sent her a second ring. Many months later, she found the first ring, so she now had two rings from me, which she eventually soldered together. I attempted to obtain a visitor's visa on several occasions, but was unsuccessful. Because of the Palestinian uprising against the Israeli occupation of the Palestinian Territories, which lasted from 1987 to 1993, and after Desert Storm, there was no way a young, Middle Eastern male would be given a visitor's visa. Eventually I asked Carrie to fly to Jordan, along with Änna. Carrie said yes and, the night before she was to travel, told her mother.

Her mother was inconsolable and told her that if Carrie and Änna went to Jordan, they would never return to the U.S. She pleaded with Carrie to think about her child's life, if not her own life. This was soon after the release of the movie, *Not Without My Daughter.* Carrie was sufficiently frightened by her mother to not go to Jordan. Bassem went to Carrie's apartment the day of the scheduled flight, and called her many times on the building intercom. He asked her to let him in as he had the tickets and he was going to drive them to the airport. Carrie panicked and would not open the door. As testament to my brother Bassem's kind heart, he never held this against Carrie in the future.

A few days later, Carrie spoke with me over the phone. I told her, "I understand why you didn't come. I understand why you were scared. I will give you one more chance and will send you another ticket. If you don't come this time, don't bother contacting me ever again."

Unbeknownst to Carrie, I had sold my treasured car to be able to buy the plane tickets for her and Änna. I had to sell yet another car to purchase another ticket.

Carrie recognized the seriousness in my voice when I gave her one more chance. She did not take it lightly.

As Carrie was now out of college and had been generously supported by her parents, she knew that she must become independent for the next stage of her life. She also knew that, if she moved forward with marrying me, all assistance from her parents would stop immediately.

She found a cheap apartment in another part of the city. Her aunt and uncle (the uncle who worked for Billy Graham Evangelistic Association) came and helped her move to the new apartment. She worked part-time in an Arabic restaurant and began to diligently seek full-time work. Her uncle proposed that she apply to BGEA's legal department. She did so, and was offered a job beginning December 1992.

She talked with her good friend, Valerie (my brother Bassem's former girlfriend). Valerie told Carrie she would stay with Änna if Carrie decided to travel to Jordan and marry me. Valerie had been good friends with Barhoum, and she knew all the history surrounding Carrie's relationship with him, as well as life with the Tahtamouni family. To this day, Carrie doesn't know why Valerie supported her in traveling to Jordan to get married.

At this time, it was Thanksgiving. Carrie was to travel home with Änna to spend the holiday on the farm with her parents. Instead, she went to the airport and boarded a plane for Jordan, and Valerie stayed with Änna. After Carrie was safely on her way and had gotten as far as Amsterdam, Valerie called Carrie's parents and told them that Carrie had traveled to Jordan. Carrie's parents immediately came to pick up Änna.

Marriage

My father, my sister, and I met Carrie when she landed in Jordan. It was a very emotional meeting. In part this was because it was the first time we were meeting Carrie and she was meeting us, and in part because we all keenly felt the loss of Barhoum and knew how much he would have been overjoyed at our meeting. He had often written to Carrie of his desire for her and Änna to visit Jordan and meet our parents and all his family. My father and sister hugged Carrie. She paused in front of me, held out her hand, and then I spontaneously hugged her. There were not many words, as we were not fluent in English and Carrie was not fluent in Arabic. Yet there was a sense of this moment being significant and we all had tears in our eyes. Carrie later said she was immediately struck by the kindness in my eyes. I was tall, six feet, and extremely thin. My thinness made me seem taller than I actually was. And I had an enormous mustache that seemingly overtook my narrow face. We drove from the airport in the capital of Amman to our family home in a nearby city.

After eating a delicious meal of mensaf, a traditional dish of lamb and cooked yogurt claimed by both Palestinians and Jordanians, we sat in the living room and stayed up all night talking. Our talking was somewhat stilted, as I was not fluent in English and Carrie knew very little Arabic. In the morning, my father said his attorney had found a judge who would be willing to give us permission to marry. This was quite a feat because Carrie was in a Muslim country without a male relative to give permission for her marriage. The attorney said that we must go see the judge right away. So we called a taxi and traveled to the Islamic courthouse in the ancient city of Jerash.

The attorney, my father, and I went in to see the judge. Carrie sat out in a cold, dark, wide hallway or courtyard with chairs on either side. There was a woman and her child on the opposite side. Suddenly, my father came out and escorted Carrie to the other side, as she had inadvertently sat on the men's side of the hallway. After some time, my father came out again and took her in to see the judge. The judge had told the attorney that he would marry us, but only if the marriage took place immediately. If we would not marry immediately, he would not consider marrying us in the future. Before we knew it, we were standing in front of the judge. He spoke in Arabic and asked Carrie to repeat what he said to the best of her ability. Carrie did not understand a word of what was being said. Then the judge pronounced us married.

In Jordan, the homes are made of concrete and my family home did not have central heat. We carry kerosene heaters called *sopas* from room to room. We were married on a rainy November day and it was very damp and very cold. Carrie was chilled to the very bone. When we returned to the house, it was as if it was a normal day in the life of the household. Because Carrie had not slept for two days, she was escorted to a bedroom, where she slept all day. In the evening, I woke her up and we ate dinner with the family. While my family was still in mourning over the death of my brother Barhoum, it was still very crushing for Carrie because no one said congratulations. No mention was really made of our marriage. My brother, Nabil, would not give his permission when I requested to go to the capital, Amman, to spend the night. That was that. There was no celebration, no special meal, no congratulatory wishes. There were no photos taken of us on our wedding day. It was a dismal launch into married life.

Money was tight at this time, as the cost of my brothers' education and living expenses in America had greatly drained my family financially. Further, after the first Iraq war, Desert Storm, Jordan was flooded with Iraqi refugees as well as Jordanians and Palestinians who had been living and working in Kuwait and Iraq. This negatively affected the Jordanian economy. It was unthinkable to go to a hotel in the same city as my family, as it would be considered a shame not to stay with one's family. As my city is a smaller and more conservative city than the capital, Amman, there was far more to see and do in Amman. A typical wedding involves renting a party space in a restaurant or hotel, catering food, and gifts of clothing, gold, and jewelry. My family was simply not in a position to host a wedding, either monetarily or emotionally. Finally, my brother Nabil, even though he was only one year older than me, carried the power and authority of the family as he had taken over the running of my father's business. He essentially had final say on family decisions. While he has a kind heart, he can appear as harsh and unfriendly at first. This is how Carrie perceived him. Carrie cried for years after this because of how my family treated our marriage. She could visibly see the pain and loss my mother was struggling with. Carrie's heart went out to my mother because she, too, was experiencing the loss of Barhoum. But she was crushed by the cold reception Nabil gave her and our marriage. Carrie jokes to this day that she was the Tahtamouni family's American bargain.

Carrie says that, while she had loved Barhoum, she had always had mistrust or fear of what life would be like with him. But the moment she became my wife, she felt safe and protected. She knew in her heart that I was kind and that I would take care of her and Änna, no matter what. While she did not know me at all, in that we had just met, she felt that it was right for her to marry me and that I was the husband God intended for her. At the same time, she was certain that, after talking with me and spending time with me, I would become a Christian as Barhoum had done. She did not know that I was not my brother and I would not be moved in this regard, period. I was a Muslim and I would remain a Muslim!

My sister, Tamara, brought Carrie a skirt and a beautiful sweater and coat. She also invited us to Amman for an evening with her and her husband. They took us to an amazing dinner buffet with a singer, Malham Barakat, and dancing. Outside the restaurant, there was a Bedouin tent where we sat while waiting to go inside. We do have a photo from this night. My sister and her husband were the only ones to recognize our marriage in any significant way, and we will always be grateful to them for this.

I took my bride sightseeing to the Dead Sea, Hama, Ajloun, and to various places in Amman and Jordan Valley. We had a whirlwind ten days together, and then it was time for Carrie to return to Änna in America.

Carrie's parents picked her up at the airport. They were very stoic and cold. Shirley finally asked her, "What did you do in Jordan?" Carrie responded that she had gotten married. Her parents did not say much, dropped Carrie and Änna at their apartment, and returned to the family farm.

Carrie immediately started work at BGEA. The workday opened with quiet time and prayer, and Carrie decided to read the book, *Good Morning Holy Spirit,* by Benny Hinn. The book greatly impacted her desire to walk more closely with the Lord. This just after going to Jordan and marrying a Muslim! What was she thinking?

With the assistance of an attorney at a social service agency that assisted refugee and low-income clients, Carrie completed the necessary paperwork to bring me to the United States. After six months, my application was approved and I arrived on June 10, 1993, which happened to be Carrie's mother's birthday.

Coming to America

I arrived in the U.S. with $5 in my pocket. Carrie picked me up at the airport and took me to her new apartment. Through her friend Valerie, who worked for a property management company, Carrie secured a job as caretaker for an apartment building that allowed for reduced rent. My brother Bassem had taken a summer internship for a local company. I started out the new chapter in my life, as husband and instant father, in a new country completely culturally different from my own, while sharing an apartment with Carrie, Änna, and my brother.

It was very tight financially, and we had only one car (courtesy of Carrie's father). Through my brother's internship and his company connections, I was able to get a job as a machine operator in an expanded metal factory. This was a huge blessing because my English skills were minimal and I had only a high school education. This was because my parents had run out of funds when it came time for me to enter college. It was a tough, greasy job, the men were not overly friendly, and there were the typical camel jockey jokes, references to my *Jewish* cousins, asking if I grew up in a tent, whether people had televisions or electricity, and whether Arabs drive or only ride camels and donkeys (apparently my co-workers had never heard of Arabian horses). When a co-worker told me to dump the solvent, I didn't know where to dispose of it, so I dumped it in the toilet. I quickly found out that this was *not* okay, and I never forgot how to dispose of it going forward!

I did not know the language proficiently (I had studied British English, not American English), I was new to American culture, and I did not really know Carrie at all. These aspects, combined with the sudden responsibility of being a father and sharing tight quarters with my brother, contributed to our life together getting off to a bumpy start. There were lots of misunderstandings, due, in part, to a basic inability to understand one another, both language-wise and culturally. On the bright side, my brother made a good translator when things were at their worst. Änna also struggled in this new home because she suddenly had a father for the first time in her life, and she also had a full-time uncle (Bassem had been present in her life for special occasions such as birthdays but he had not been with her continuously).

Through it all, Carrie's parents helped us time and time again, and we would not have made it without their assistance and the safety net they provided. They helped pay for Änna's daycare. Because I would get home from work earlier than Carrie, I would bus home from work, pick up Änna, and then carry her on my shoulders for the mile-plus walk home. These were special times for us.

The first time I traveled to the farm to meet Carrie's parents, Shirley and I visited together in the kitchen. I said to her, "I suppose you want to know why I married your daughter." She said yes, she would like to know. I told her, "Änna needed a father and that is why I married your daughter." Shirley didn't say anything at the time, but we have talked about this conversation many times since. She tells me how much this honesty meant to her and how she quickly learned to like and respect me. While we never had arguments or disagreements, I would often get frustrated because I felt she was a little bossy. However, I knew she was motivated by her love for Carrie, so I accepted it. Some examples of my frustrations include specific seating arrangements at the table when we visited the farm, insisting on holding hands while praying before meals, specific bed times when visiting, planning the entire day and implementing a full schedule, often including getting together with family and friends without consulting me first; sharing something I was thankful for before eating the Thanksgiving meal, and the dreaded family picture at Christmas. Many of these issues are typical of any relationship between son-in-law and mother-in-law. But more than that, Arabs do not like schedules or bed times! Shirley did show me respect by not preparing any pork when we visited. However, this may have been a response to my threat not to visit if she served pork to me or my family. I love Shirley very much and appreciate her for putting up with me over the many years. Shirley now tells everyone that I'm her favorite son-in-law. Of course, I'm her only son-in-law!

I immediately got along with Carrie's father, David. He was always quiet and, if he would choose to speak, he was nice and kind to me. He has always supported me and showed me respect. I was immediately impressed by the sincerity of David's faith. He would not work on Sunday, he did not drink alcohol, and he would not grow barley because beer was made from it. He was an honest man, a man of his word. He treated me with respect because that is how he treats all those he is involved with; he did not treat me differently than he treated others because of my heritage or religion. I liked to go with him to the farm shop and he allowed me to drive his big Ford tractor. I cultivated a field for him once, but I had a lot of gaps and missed a lot of areas. He humorously thanked me by saying, "Thanks for not killing the weeds," and he had to redo the entire field. I also liked to assist him in his recycling business when I would visit (David started recycling in his county and Shirley visited all the area schools to educate and encourage children to recycle), riding with him on the recycling truck, baling recycled paper, and driving his truck in the local July parade. I couldn't ask for a better father-in-law.

Carrie's parents gave us a wedding party at their home, which was attended by close friends and relatives. In August, after Carrie had been at BGEA only nine months, the attorney who helped her complete my immigrant paperwork asked her to work at the same social service agency. This was a wonderful experience for us, as this agency puts on an amazing international festival each year. This festival celebrates the immigrants who have made the city what it is today and includes a U.S. citizenship swearing in ceremony. We met many wonderful people while Carrie worked there. She began carpooling with a co-worker and I now drove to work. I had an international driver's license when I first arrived in the U.S. I was able to pass the driver's test the second time and I received a state driver's license, for which I was thankful.

After a year, we were able to buy our first home in the north part of the city, a 1920 story-and-a-half stucco home. I did quite a bit of work on the house with David's help. Part of the reason we chose that particular neighborhood was because, with David and Shirley's assistance, Änna was starting kindergarten at a private Christian school.

Carrie had been attending Living Word, pastored by Mac Hammond, off and on since moving to the area. She knew they had a school and she hoped to send Änna there. It was somewhat of an ordeal applying to the school, because I was not a Christian and Carrie had to explain this situation in the application. I was not against Änna attending the school. I believed that Christians had better values than the general American population, so I thought it would be a good place for Änna to be. And it was. It was an excellent school.

Änna excelled in school and proved to be very bright. I would attend school events and I even attended church occasionally with Carrie and Änna. However, one night Carrie brought me to hear Billye Brim who was speaking at Living Word. She talked about Israel, about the Jewish people as well as Muslims, and that hell was a real destination. I walked out, smoked a cigarette, and told Carrie I was never going back.

Our daughter, Marina, was born during a March blizzard in 1995. Änna was so excited to go to kinder-garten the next day and tell her classmates that she had a sister. Änna was never jealous or unkind. She was very loving to her new sister. Marina brought us so much joy as she was a very happy baby, with red, round cheeks. When she was about a year old, we picked her up from daycare at our next-door-neighbor's home. Our neighbor excitedly called us in and said, "Marina's hair is going to be curly!" She wound Marina's hair around a pencil to form a ringlet and the ringlet stayed in place. Sure enough, Marina grew a full, thick head of dark, beautiful curls. She also loved to sing and still does. We love to tell the story of Marina singing a song from a Disney movie at age three. She would sing at the top of her lungs with her mouth open so wide we could see her tonsils quiver.

In July 1995, thanks to encouragement from the director at Carrie's workplace, our family traveled to Jordan. It was the first time my family had met Änna, and my mother was overcome with emotion. She had Änna sleep with her every night and it was a very special time for her. All the family could clearly see Änna's resemblance to Barhoum, especially from her nose down to her chin. People who meet Änna today, who knew her father, say she looks nearly exactly like him, especially her teeth and her smile. While we were in Jordan, we did some sightseeing. My mother would have preferred that Änna not go sightseeing but rather stay next to her side. This was not out of control, but out of a deep satisfaction of having Änna near her. After Barhoum's death, my mom's hair went from gray to completely white and she was never the same again, either health-wise or emotionally. My mother had been very close to Barhoum. She derived great comfort from seeing and spending time with Änna. We had many special times as a family in Jordan. My mother and sister planned a party for Änna's seventh birthday, two months prior to Änna's actual birthday. My mother gave Änna gold earrings and a bracelet and other family members gave her gold as well as other beautiful gifts. Various family members also brought gifts of gold for Carrie. It is typical for families in the Middle East to give gold as gifts because it can be turned into money when necessary. We all sat in the front yard, under grape vines that created a shaded canopy. My mother had Änna on her lap much of the time. We visited my father's sister in the Jordan Valley where she prepared a huge meal. We had a family barbecue in a little town called Melka, on the mountain across from the Golan Heights, looking down at the Sea of Galilee. We visited the Dead Sea, Rabat castle, and the ancient city of Petra. My mother did not accompany us on any of the sightseeing, but encouraged her children and grand-children to go. Carrie and I have often talked of how my parents walked outside and down to the street to wave goodbye to us. My mother stood outside and waved to us. This was the last time Carrie, Änna and Marina saw my mother.

When we returned from Jordan, we kept busy with work and our children. We began to develop friendships with other Arab Muslim families, whereas prior to vis-iting Jordan we had mostly kept to ourselves. We were blessed to find a daycare provider right on our block for Marina, and Änna was a busy, serious student. The neighbors were generally pretty friendly and we would sometimes meet on the sidewalk and chat. A common topic was the increasing crime. It seemed to be getting worse rather quickly. Änna would hear gunfire after going to bed, would get frightened, and would run to our room. I tried to calm her by suggesting that it could have been fireworks. After hearing gunfire sporadically each week, and after having our trash cans painted with gang symbols twice, as well as being set on fire, we decided it was time to move. In 1997, we sold our house for a profit and purchased a home in a suburb of the city.

If ever someone were to land in an idyllic neighborhood, this was it. All the neighbors knew one another, had a yearly block party, looked out for one another and were just good, hard-working, kind people. We still keep in touch with several of these neighbors today.

Carrie's program at the social service agency was phased out, so the director sent her to work for his wife, a curator of a special children's book collection, at a large state university. I continued to work at the factory but was quickly moving up. I asked to learn how to run every machine on the floor. And whenever we received new jobs and new machines, I asked to learn how to run the new jobs and the new machines. My co-workers thought I was crazy, asking for more work, and sometimes more difficult work. I enjoyed the challenge. Soon I was promoted to a lead position, and eventually to management.

Änna turned out to be a super achiever and she would work herself to perfection. The stress went to her stomach and she was often ill. The school provided excellent Christian education. The staff and students were fantastic and the standards they set were very high. We decided to send Änna to a Catholic school near Carrie's work. She did very well there academically, but she felt a lot of pressure as the only Protestant in her classroom. Her teacher was particularly hard on her the day she outscored all of her Catholic classmates on a Catechism test.

After much discussion, we decided to send Änna to public school in our district. We did not know how we could provide private school for a second child when we were only able to provide it for Änna with Carrie's parents' assistance. This neighborhood school was wonderful and we have many wonderful memories there.

I was not a practicing Muslim throughout this time. I never had been diligent about performing the duties required by Islam. I had started smoking at age thirteen. The more addicted I became to smoking, the more difficult it was to fast at Ramadan because the observance requires no eating, drinking or smoking, from sunrise to sunset. I just couldn't go without smoking for that long.

When Änna entered third grade, I announced that she would no longer be able to wear shorts. This was hard for Änna and for Carrie. While Carrie dressed conservatively, and I had no issues with her clothing, I was fiercely protective of Änna. Based on how I had seen women dress in America – even in church, when I had attended with Carrie – I refused to let Änna grow up with such immodesty. I was also very strict about where Änna went and with whom. While I was happy for Änna to have her friends over at our home, I would not allow Änna to stay at her friends' homes. To this day, Änna is still crushed that I did not allow her to attend her best friend's golden birthday party and sleepover held at a local hotel. Änna tells me, "Who does that, Dad?" We do have many happy memories of Änna's friends hanging out at our home and even traveling with us, so there were some good times, despite my strict parenting.

My mother-in-law was very concerned about the fact that I was not a U.S. citizen. She, too, heard all the stories about Middle Eastern men marrying American women for the green card. I think she may have thought that if I was a citizen, there would be more security for Carrie and Änna. Whatever her reasons, she got the U.S. citizenship study materials and told me she was coming to stay with me and help me prepare for the test. Study we did! I was not into studying, but Shirley patiently persisted and thoroughly quizzed me. I went to my interview totally prepared and was granted citizenship. Both Shirley and David attended the swearing-in ceremony. They took a photo of me with the judge, which I have until this day.

My mother was not feeling well and was eventually diagnosed with colon cancer. Carrie and her parents encouraged me to go to Jordan to visit my mother. I traveled there in March 1998. Shirley came to stay with Carrie and the girls. Shirley tells how Marina would ask her, "When is my father coming home?" Marina developed a stutter while I was away that disappeared when I returned from Jordan. It was very traumatic for her to be away from me. But I'm so glad I went and saw my mother one more time.

My mother was always concerned about her children and grandchildren. I had spoken to her on the phone and mentioned that Marina had a fever. My mom called the next day to inquire as to whether Marina was better. She would also call me if she had a dream or sensed that something was wrong. She was attentive and loving to me at all times.

My mother's condition required surgery. The surgery went well. The doctor believed they had caught it early and had gotten all the cancer. However, my mother did not get up and walk like she should have after surgery. For this reason, she developed pneumonia and died suddenly of a heart attack.

Bassem called me in the middle of the night to tell me that our mother had died. It was a shock and it devastated me and Bassem. By this time, Carrie and I had made quite a few friendships with other Muslim families throughout the city. I began receiving condolence calls. Carrie's parents came, along with her brother and his wife, and Muslim friends brought food and gave their sympathy. We were appreciative of this kindness shown by our friends and family.

After this, I decided I had better get serious about Allah. I began to pray five times a day. I also began to get quite strict with Carrie and the girls. While we never would eat pork nor have pork in our home, I would celebrate Christmas with Carrie's family at their home and Carrie would decorate for the holiday as well. I had been fine with Carrie going to church with Änna. Now I put my foot down and told her that she could go, but Änna was not allowed to go. Thus began many years of stress and strain on our marriage and much pain for our children. This pain was not so much a result of not celebrating American Christian holidays; it was more to do with the division in our home. Neither Carrie nor I agree with the commercialization or extravagances displayed by many American families in relation to these holidays.

Prior to my mother's death, we had planned to bring my parents to the U.S. to visit. When my mother died, we brought my father to the U.S. to live with us. Carrie loved my father very much and was in agreement with this plan. But I cracked down harder at home because I could not have my father see that my wife attended church or that I allowed her to celebrate Christian holidays. And while I had gone along with Christmas in the past, Easter was an absolute no in my home. To say that Jesus had died and rose again from the dead was blasphemy! And to celebrate his resurrection with ham – are you crazy? So Carrie didn't dare do a thing for

Easter. It was a non-event at our house, although I did let her go to church with her parents if we happened to be at their home for the holiday.

About this time, Carrie was contacted by the attorney who prepared the paperwork to bring me to the United States. She had left the non-profit agency when funding ran out for the legal program, and had entered corporate America. She asked Carrie to come work as her assistant for a computer software company that had its own in-house green card department. Carrie loved immigration and was excited to join her friend at this new company.

Arab families love to gather together and we met many Muslim families through the dinners and picnics we attended. We worked hard all week and then socialized all weekend. Arabs are famous for their wonderful hospitality. It is serious business and it consumed much of our lives. We would visit families and then they would visit us. They would invite us for meals and we would invite them for meals. Carrie entered into the cultural aspects and worked very hard at being a good wife. She picked up on a lot of Arabic, cooked Arabic food, and did her best to fit in. But she always felt that, as an American, she never measured up.

If there is competition regarding who is the best cook between American wives, multiply that by 100 with Arabic women. Wherever Carrie went, she felt the competition about who was the best cook, who had the nicest house, who had the smartest kids, who had the most lavish parties, who was the best Muslim, who had the most gold, and on and on it went. Many times, Carrie would cry all the way home after attending one of these gatherings. While she genuinely loved these women and developed several close friendships, she could feel an undercurrent of dislike for her on the part of some women.

While most of our family friends were Arab Muslims, we had some American friends as well. I had American friends through work and would attend football games, tailgate parties, and boating on the lake. While some Americans were suspicious of my Middle Eastern background, the majority of the people I dealt with had open minds and enjoyed learning about a different culture. While people would not necessarily say anything, I could feel when I was not accepted by them. Overall, however, the Americans I have met are welcoming and accepting and we have wonderful American and Arab Muslim friends. Ultimately, people are the same everywhere and there are wonderful and not-so-wonderful people in every country and culture.

Carrie had always wanted a large family. Her father came from a family of eight, and Carrie had only one brother. She always felt that a large family had more love and more adventure and she prayed and prayed for another baby. In fact, she had prayed and prayed for Marina (who arrived after we were married two years). And now she had been praying and praying for another child. She would often cry and ask, "Why isn't God giving us another baby?" I was never concerned about it. Two girls were fine with me. But Carrie not only wanted more children, she greatly desired a son. I was truly happy with my girls and did not feel any pressure to have a son. While I would have liked a son, it was not a burning desire for me.

Part of this was because of all the stories she heard from our Muslim friends about women who couldn't have children or, specifically, sons, so their husbands took another wife. One time we were talking and calculated that nine out of ten of our closest Arab Muslim family friends had married American women, received their green cards, divorced their American wives, went back to the Middle East to marry a second time, and then brought their Muslim wives to America. Carrie felt that American women were used by Muslim men as free green card passes and then disposed of when they were no longer useful, in favor of women from their own culture who would keep immaculate homes, cook lavish meals, wait on their husbands, host fabulous parties and bear them many sons. Carrie felt that she was looked upon as second class, as someone whose husband would eventually divorce her for a better bride from back home and that she would never measure up to expected Arab Muslim standards. She would cook and clean and go to parties and host parties but she was never fully accepted. She also keenly felt the fact that she did not have a son. Carrie always wondered in the back of her mind if I would leave her, and she thought that if she could at least give me a son, there would be less risk. I think this also related to the fact that she knew that ultimately I had married her because of Änna and not because I loved her. I made a decision to

93

marry her and I grew to love her, but initially I married her because of Änna. So these were underlying issues in our marriage and in our relationship.

Not only was this social competition emotionally draining on our family, it was also financially draining. As our Arab Muslim friends became more and more successful, they would throw more and more elaborate parties. Soon they were inviting forty people to a restaurant for Ramadan breakfast. And soon an expected birthday gift for one of their children was a minimum of $50. I had also purchased gold for Carrie over the years for her birthday or other special occasions, following the traditions of my culture. We quickly became bogged down in debt as we tried to keep up with our friends.

The positive side of our involvement with these Arab Muslim families is that our children were exposed to two cultures and learned some of the rich and beautiful traditions of the Middle East. These included standing up to respectfully greet others, especially elders, by either shaking hands or hugging and kissing the cheeks; by addressing those older than them as *aunt* or *uncle*, by giving up their place to allow someone older than them to sit comfortably, and how to offer hospitality to unexpected guests and generosity to those who are struggling or in need.

While there were many wonderful times with our friends, it could also be hard on our children. The topic at many of these parties was Islam, how many times a day one prayed, whether one followed all the rules, whether the women wore hijab, and who went to the mosque most frequently. I commanded our kids to say, if anyone asked, that they were Muslim. And Carrie wouldn't say a thing. I was the head of the house, they were my children, and they were Muslim. End of story.

Carrie told me that Islam means "Submission to God," and that, as a Christian, she was submitted to God, so it was not dishonest to call herself a Muslim. This twisted concept gave her some mental relief from the strain she was experiencing in our home and helped her walk a fine line and continue to compromise so our marriage would not fall apart.

In 2000, we learned we were expecting again. This was an answer to many, many prayers on Carrie's part. At the ultrasound, we learned we were having a girl with unusually large feet. I cried. Carrie thought it was

because we were having another girl and not the cov-
eted son. She was livid the entire day and I think she
still is. She was thrilled to be having another child. In
July, we were blessed with another daughter. I named
her Aisha, after my mother. While Marina was excited
for a new baby brother or sister, and had often prayed
earnestly with her mother during bedtime prayers for
a new sibling, Aisha's birth brought about a change in
her. She was no longer the happy, joyful child she was
before. Because there was a five-year gap between
Marina and Aisha, my only explanation is that Marina
felt she lost her place somehow when Aisha was born.

That same year, I enrolled Änna and Marina in
summer school at a local mosque so they could learn
more about Islam. One day, when I picked the girls up,
Änna was sobbing. I asked her why. She told me that
the instructor had told her that her mother was going
to hell because she was a Christian. I did not send the
girls back to the school after that.

At home and in our marriage, we tried to focus on
our similarities, not our differences. We would discuss
God, moral values, and modesty with our girls. But I
would not allow the name of Jesus to be spoken unless

I used it when swearing. I did not swear often, but when I did, that was the name I used.

The General Counsel at Carrie's company suffered a stroke and the entire atmosphere at the company changed. He had been like a loving father to the entire legal department and his absence was keenly felt. While he survived the stroke, he was never able to work again. He had been a pilot and traveled a lot, both domestically and internationally for work and pleasure. It was devastating to see his life turn upside down so quickly. He was only in his fifties at the time. He continued his zest for life even though his circumstances had dramatically changed and life had become a continual struggle. He passed away a number of years later. This affected me a lot. He was kind to me the first time I met him. He welcomed me to his home. When I would go to Carrie's office, he would greet me and visit with me. He would ask me how I was doing and really cared about my life. This was different from the other attorneys, who didn't have the time of day for me. As a Muslim, I believed that only those who confessed Mohammad as their prophet could go to heaven. Yet I struggled with the idea that, according to Islam, this man might be in hell when I recalled his kindness, generosity, and goodness. When I learned of his death, it made me think more about Islam and what I had been taught. It also caused me to think that there had to be more answers.

In part because of the long commute, Carrie left the company and began to work for one of the oldest law firms in the state. Between jobs, we decided to take a quick family trip. We flew to Orlando, Florida with the entire family. It was a highlight for all of us. One morning in our hotel room, Aisha started choking and turning blue. Carrie called 9-1-1. She was screaming because she could see that Aisha had a foil fruit roll-up wrapper halfway down her throat and she was struggling to breathe. I took Aisha in my arms and tried to pull the wrapper out. By the time the ambulance arrived, Aisha had been able to swallow the wrapper and subsequently breathe and get enough oxygen. It was a terrible scare.

That September was the infamous Nine-Eleven. I was home sick that day, but felt well enough to drive Carrie to work downtown, as she usually took the bus. On the drive there, we heard on the radio the first report of the plane hitting the tower. The law firm closed before noon that morning, and I headed back to pick Carrie up. We were glued to the television all day, as was all of America. When I returned to work the next day, many comments were made asking where I was and hinting at the possibility that I was involved in some way.

A couple days after the attack, we went to visit our closest Muslim friends. It was a tense time because of the emotions surrounding the attack and the talk of Islamic perpetrators. At the end of the evening, my friend's wife suddenly started shouting, saying that she would gladly give a son as a martyr for Islam. Carrie was shocked and horrified because she had not meant to trigger anything by an earlier comment (which she no longer recalls). At any rate, this close friendship was essentially terminated in an instant. We have never been close since, although we still occasionally visit one another. We had been with this family weekly, sometimes several times a week, for several years. How quickly things changed.

September eleventh drastically changed not only our friendships and our country but also our marriage relationship. Carrie read more about Islam and dug into the how and why of what would cause people to do what they did. She had always had a keen sense of justice and she was almost addicted to researching this issue and would dwell on it incessantly. This drove me crazy, as I felt she was always hammering me and my religion. I didn't support terrorism, but I felt that she was barking at me all the time.

Another close Muslim friend babysat Marina and Aisha, as well as Änna when Änna had school breaks or during summer vacation. Aisha was actually fluent in Arabic because our friend spoke only Arabic with her. This woman is one of Carrie's dearest friends to this day. When we would get together, the terrorist attack would often come up in conversation.

This same friend also babysat a little boy named Marwan. He had the most beautiful eyes I have ever seen. In fact, his eyes were so powerful, I would feel I couldn't continue to look in them and I would look away. His nature was so sweet that our friend would say he was like an angel and we all agreed. I had met Marwan's father, Sami, approximately a year earlier when he purchased a business that I frequented. I had met

Sami's cousin in 1993 as he had a restaurant near the apartment we were living in. Sami and I quickly became friends and I consider him one of my dearest friends. Sami is kind, generous, understanding, loyal and he does not gossip about others. If someone angers him, he says, *Insa,* meaning *forget it, forgive, let go.*

In 2002, when Aisha was two-and-a-half, we traveled to Jordan again. This time it was to visit my mother's grave, and Änna went to see her father's grave. We traveled there at the end of Ramadan. It was a good opportunity for the girls to experience Eid (the celebration after the month of Ramadan fasting) in a Muslim country. While we would celebrate Eid with our Muslim friends in the U.S. by buying new clothes, going to prayer, visiting one another, and congregating at the mall, I wanted my children to see what it was like celebrating Eid in Jordan. We stayed nearly three weeks and were able to visit many places, including Petra and Aqaba. It was a wonderful trip – but we keenly felt the absence of my mother.

We returned to America. The next year we learned we were expecting again. Carrie had closely followed suggestions from Arab friends and family about how to conceive a male child. My father had offered many prayers that, insha allah, we would have a son.

In July 2002, I received a SOS call from my brother Nabil, in Jordan. He believed that he was being targeted by a militant Palestinian Islamic group that wanted him to join them and work for them. When Nabil refused to become a member, he was under surveillance, was chased, had to hide at various locations, and a kidnap attempt was made on his son. I sent funds to him and Carrie prepared visa invitation paperwork in an attempt to get him to the U.S. as a visitor (she did not realize that he was in grave danger at the time, as I had not shared all the details at that point). Miraculously, his visa was approved and he arrived shortly after. He lived with us and worked for a Muslim Arab at his grocery store. One night his boss asked him to come to the store to assist him in closing. When Nabil arrived, his boss had been shot and was dead. I knew, as my brother knew, that his life was miraculously spared. If he would have gotten to the store an instant sooner, he would have died as well. This murder was in the media and I was interviewed by a local television station.

My dedication to prayer five times a day had not lasted overly long after my mother's death. After this incident, I renewed my former resolution to pray as required. Carrie, believing that tuning into God, even if it was the Muslim God and not her Christian savior, felt that it was better than not paying attention to God at all. So she went to a local store and purchased me a new prayer rug with a compass so I could pray towards Mecca. Again, my renewed commitment to pray did not last too long.

Things had gotten very bad financially. We had been living way beyond our means. We had redone nearly every square inch of the house we were living in – from the roof to the basement. The projects always ended up costing more than anticipated (our initial plan was to fix this house and sell it for profit like our first home). Combined with the trips to Jordan, the social obligations with our Muslim friends, and having three children, we were ready to implode. I had been able to make all my payments and keep up with everything, but the stress was overwhelming. I had already had a wake-up call with pneumonia, possible heart issues, and a long hospital stay. I was hardly keeping it together.

Throughout our married years, whenever really serious problems would arise with job changes, financial situations, or child-rearing issues, I would call Carrie's parents and ask them for advice and prayer. I would also call and talk to Agnes. She would always give me solid advice that I could count on.

In September 2003, God blessed us with a son. I named him Sayfaldin, which means *sword of religion.* My name means *sword* and my nickname growing up had been Abu Sayf, *father of the sword.* So I always said that if I had a son, I would name him Sayf. Carrie agreed to Sayfaldin because, in her mind, it meant *sword of faith*, which had great spiritual meaning to her. Although I was adamant that all my children would have Arabic first names, I compromised with Carrie and let her choose the second name. We both agreed on *David* as Sayf's second name. By the time Sayf was one, he had a full head of thick, white-blond curls. It was hard to believe I was the father, as Sayf looked like he was directly from Norway.

We were extremely busy with work and our children. Änna participated wholeheartedly in school life, including debate, theatre, and enrolling in the

International Baccalaureate Program. She had made good friends. They were always busy with one another, doing positive things like studying, attending extracurricular events, volunteering, and working. Änna was very strong and would not give up any fight to obtain more freedom, whether it was to travel to California with her school choir, to attend a school dance, or to wear clothes that she found fashionable but I disagreed with. She would simply not give up and would often exhaust me with her tenacity. At the same time, she respected me. For the most part, we had a good relationship. There were often power struggles and there were a few all-out fights I would prefer to forget.

Marina was a good student and had several close friends. She was in swimming lessons and took to the water very well. The instructors advised that she enter competitive swimming, although Marina never desired to do so. I would have had problems with this because, as she got older, I never would have allowed her to wear a swimsuit in public. She also loved music and was involved in all-district choir and orchestra, as was Änna before her. Marina also loved animals and was always asking for us to get a dog. This was awkward, because my father lived with us and, according to Islam, dogs are considered filthy. Amazingly, my brother who was most strict about religion, Nabil, gifted Marina with a beautiful Siberian Husky. Unfortunately, the dog tried to bite the neighbor boy when the boy was tossing a Frisbee to Marina, and we had to give the dog to the authorities.

Aisha was a very happy child, always talking and singing to herself and often disappearing into her room to play. She would become very agitated, however, if her routine was upset. We have learned that she is borderline ADD. She is able to self-regulate by writing notes and lists to herself and keeping on a regular schedule with homework and school routines. Aisha loves to do well and please others, and makes friends easily. She is also very kind and helpful to her parents and siblings.

Through very hard life lessons, we learned that we could only live on our salaries. All credit cards were terminated and we were living on a very tight budget. We absolutely could not keep up with our Arab friends because we had no funds to do so, so we quietly withdrew nearly completely from our former friendships and activities.

The founder of Carrie's law firm was a Christian. Past protocol was to give each new employee a Bible. This was not true anymore, but several employees at the firm reserved a room each Friday at noon and met to pray. They prayed for fellow employees and for one another. Carrie would come home and tell me about different prayer needs and then she would tell me about answers to those prayers. I also met each member of the prayer group and their husbands. I was impacted by their integrity and faith in God. As this group was very small, approximately five women, they became very close. Carrie was particularly close to one of the women, Winifred. This woman faithfully prayed for my salvation and for our family. She was a great encouragement to Carrie.

We were able to bring my dad's sister, affectionately called *Amti* (*aunt* in Arabic), my sister, and two of her children to the U.S. in 2005. This is the aunt I lived with during the civil war in Jordan. We still laugh about Amti and the commotion she caused in our quiet neighborhood. She would wash her hair and comb olive oil in it. She would wear her long, Palestinian dress and sit on the ground in the front corner of our lawn. Amti and my father, in his pajamas, would sit on a bench in front of the house and smoke together. Amti would not let Carrie wash any of her clothes, but she would hang her underwear out to dry for all the neighbors to see. We went sightseeing around the city one time. Amti found grape leaves growing near the river and she gathered as many as she could in her long skirt. We had quite a feast that night!

My friend Sami's son was very ill with cancer and did not have long to live. It was tragic, especially as Marwan would have started kindergarten that fall. In fact, Marwan's last wish was that his parents would buy him a backpack with school supplies so he could feel like he was going to school, even though he knew he was dying. Sami's son was the same age as our daughter Aisha, so his death touched a raw chord in me. I was at the mosque after he died and I'll never forget the sight of his little body. Marwan's heartbreaking death was another wake-up call as to how quickly death can come. It made me treasure my children more when I thought about how short life is and how powerful God is.

One of the women in Carrie's prayer group at work mentioned that a former terrorist, Walid Shoebat, was speaking at a conference held at a local church. Carrie attended the conference with her friend and noted the extra security presence in the church. This was due to the fact that Mr. Shoebat had converted from Islam to Christianity and there was concern about possible repercussions from local Muslims. Afterwards, she went up to Mr. Shoebat, told him she was married to a Muslim and that she had been praying with no results. She then asked him, "How do Muslims come to Christ?" Mr. Shoebat told her, "Through love, the love of Christ."

In 2006, I got home from work only to have Marina call out, "Dad, Jeddo needs you." *Jeddo* means *grandfather* in Arabic. I got to my dad's side and could see him sweating profusely. I immediately gave him four aspirin to chew, got him into the Suburban, and headed for the hospital. I called Carrie at work and told her that I was taking my father to a certain medical center because I had heard they take people without insurance. Carrie's work was on the way, so I picked her up from the sidewalk. My dad clutched the door handle above him all the way and didn't say a word. We got to the ER and my dad was whisked away immediately. We learned that he had suffered a heart attack and that he would need by-pass surgery. The doctor told me that the aspirin I had given my father had saved his life. My sister, Tamara, was able to come to stay with us for a month and take care of my father while Carrie and I were at work. She was completely attentive to him and slept on the floor by his side. She wouldn't leave him. Under her loving care, my father recovered very quickly.

Carrie's aunt invited her to a Women of Titus retreat at her local Baptist church. There, Carrie was challenged to read the Bible daily. She took that challenge to heart and purposed to read the entire Bible, slowly and thoroughly.

Also, around this time, she had started to diligently attend Living Word again. The secretary there told her of another woman, Sonia, who was married to a Muslim. She gave Carrie Sonia's phone number. They met and immediately became friends. Sonia is originally from Puerto Rico and her husband is originally from Iran. She wrote a book for people left behind after the rapture, *Is the Bible a Time Capsule? Is Time*

Almost Up?, and she has quite an amazing story to tell. In addition, she gave Carrie a prayer for wives to pray for unsaved husbands. Carrie prayed for me daily for months and possibly years. Carrie and Sonia would attend church together. They would call and e-mail each other whenever headline news that seemed to line up with prophetic events foretold in the Bible would take place. They continue to communicate now, and they are continuing to pray for her husband's salvation.

Missouri

~2~

I n 2006, Bassem went to work for a company in
Missouri. I had moved as far up as I could at the
company I'd been at since arriving in the United States.
I had been there over thirteen years, and there were no
more opportunities for growth. My brother's company
had an open position and he suggested that I apply. I
did so and was offered the job.

Carrie was ready for adventure and she prayed
earnestly that I would get the new job. When I did so,
we were all excited. I headed for Missouri in April and
began work. We put the house up for sale and Carrie
started packing. She prayed and prayed that the house
would sell. We had not been apart for long before, and
it was very difficult for all of us. I was allowed to fly
home periodically, but it was not frequently enough

or long enough. My son even hid my shoes one time thinking that, if I couldn't find my shoes, I wouldn't be able to leave.

The children were very upset about the move to Missouri. Änna would be a senior and had developed close friendships with her classmates. Marina, too, had many close friends and was torn up about leaving them and starting over in a new school. Aisha was a kinder-gartener, so she had not had time to put down lots of roots or make many friends. The most difficult aspect of the move, however, was leaving the neighbors. The neighbors were like family to us. They would babysit our children, would stop over for coffee or to visit, we would run into each other at school and out in the community, and they had put so much of themselves into making our neighborhood a great place to live. We were really going to miss them. And while we have lived many places since, there has not been one neighborhood as closely connected and caring as this one that we left.

After being at the company a month and having been told by the supervisor that I was doing an excellent job, I was called in and told that they were cutting my salary by $15,000. My supervisor told me that I could stay and live with it or leave. We had listed our home, Carrie had given notice at work, and our belongings were mostly packed. We made the decision to stay at the Missouri job. A Muslim Arab friend had agreed to be our realtor. Carrie had been praying for this friend and his wife's salvation. Thus far, while there had been interest in our home, we had not had any offers.

We felt like we couldn't take any more separation. Then my brother Nabil proposed that he buy our house. He would keep our father with him so as not to uproot him from his home away from home and from the Arab friends he had made. Due to my father's recent heart attack, this seemed a wise plan. A neighbor across the street would watch for my father every day as Nabil worked in a far suburb. She would watch to see that he came outside to smoke as evidence that he was awake and okay. Further, various Muslim friends in our community would stop by and take my father to Friday prayers.

I flew home for the closing, we signed the paperwork, and then we got in the vehicle and drove to Missouri. Our time in Missouri was short (only nine months) and very difficult financially. Yet God provided for us every step of the way.

My job was grueling. I worked six days a week, fourteen hours a day, second shift. I hardly saw my family. There were very few homes for rent in good condition. We found a home in the newspaper and went to visit it. There was an instant rapport with the owner of the house when we met her, and she rented it to us.

The house was located in a small town outside of a major urban area. Carrie immediately found a church – another Living Word. She took the kids there for Sunday worship services and for special events held for the youth. I didn't say too much about it because I was exhausted from working so much. She also met a lovely woman and her daughter at church, with whom Änna became good friends.

Carrie wrote a letter to every immigration attorney in the area, and was called to interview by an attorney in a town about an hour away. He hired her on the spot, over the phone. She went into the office to work once a week, and was allowed to work from home the remainder of the time. This was a blessing, as we would not have made it financially without this job. Carrie continues to work for this attorney and God has used him to provide for us financially throughout the years.

It was Änna's senior year of high school, but she took the move in stride. She worked at a clothing retailer, served as co-editor on the school newspaper, and had several close friends. Marina struggled a little, but eventually made two good friends. We had Aisha repeat kindergarten. Although she was promoted to first grade, Carrie felt that she was weak in the funda-mentals. Carrie thought, with the move to a new state, it would not be too traumatic for Aisha to repeat this grade. Sayf blissfully played at home and worked on potty-training.

Carrie would tell me things she was learning at church. Keith Moore was a guest speaker and it hap-pened that he was speaking the same time Carrie's parents came to visit us. Carrie's aunt and uncle came to visit from a nearby state when Carrie's parents were visiting. Throughout our married years, Carrie's uncle had been evangelizing me and, while I sincerely liked him, I was sick and tired of being preached at! But I enjoyed his visit. Because this aunt and uncle had been missionaries in the Middle East, they always made a point to say hello in Arabic and to discuss my culture with me.

We ate lots of rice and beans during our time in Missouri. We ate at a restaurant twice the entire time we lived there. It was tight! But we grew very close as a family. And we enjoyed being close to my brother, Bassem and his family. We spent many beautiful times together. My brother Nabil even visited us, bringing my father with him as well.

Another Move

In November, Bassem was laid off, and he and his family returned to the western state where they had lived before. Things were tight and we were lonely for family. I decided to contact a recruiter and asked him to assist me in finding a job. I told him I'd go anywhere in the United States. Christmas Day we received a call from Carrie's father, stating that her sister-in-law's brother had died on Christmas Eve. The following day, we got in the car and drove to be with Carrie's family and support them during this time of grief. On the way there, I received a telephone call from a recruiter.

He said, "There is a company interested in you, but there is one problem."

"What is it?" I asked.

When he told me, I couldn't believe it. The town was an hour from Carrie's parents' home. I said, "I'm interested."

We stopped at a McDonalds, where I received a screening call from the company itself. I told them I was coming to the area for a funeral and could interview with them while there, so an interview was scheduled.

We returned to Missouri. We were to the point where we could hardly keep up with the rent. The new company kept telling me that they wanted me, but they had not made an offer or moved forward in any way. Finally, at the end of February, they made me an offer. By March 7, we were driving to our home in a new state.

So Änna moved twice her senior year. She survived this well, but it was very hard on Marina. I don't think she ever recovered from it. While Änna is very verbal and very social, Marina is very quiet and very reserved. While Marina is blunt and says what she thinks, she is also very sensitive and easily hurt by the words of others. Quite simply, she is a beautiful but compli-cated person. Also, by this time, we learned that we were expecting again. Carrie was very sick this time

– morning sickness around the clock. We were all glad to be getting back to family.

I worked for a wind blade company based out of Denmark. While working there, I remembered that I had a vision as a young man of a large, open space, and working on huge, white things shaped like rockets. It hit me that I was working in the same place that I had seen years before.

I did well at my job supervising the weekend shift. We enjoyed seeing Carrie's parents at least once a week, sometimes more. Carrie found a church and took the kids, although I was not happy about it.

Soon after moving, Carrie took the kids to the local mall and Marina begged to visit the pet store. They all went in and Marina instantly fell in love with a little Shih Tzu puppy, all alone in his cage. Carrie was pretty taken by the puppy, too, but told Marina that she would have to talk to me and go with me to the store. Marina convinced me to take her, and Carrie's last words to me as we were leaving were, "Don't think of buying a dog unless you call and talk to me about it first." An hour later, Marina and I walked in the door with the puppy, a dish, bed, brush, and a bag of puppy food. I had not called Carrie. The girls named the dog Finn, a name they had picked out for the new baby but that I refused to consider. The family loved the dog and I intensely disliked the dog, especially as my Islamic upbringing was totally against having a dog in one's home. But I was the one who bought the dog, so I couldn't really say much. Marina's happiness was worth the stress of having a dog in the house - at least for a time.

It happened that a couple bought the house across the street from the house we were renting. They became fast friends and have remained so to this day. They run their own business and are very busy, but would always take the time to stop by in the evening or on the weekend to chat. They were particularly kind to our children, taking time to talk and joke with them, and frequently bringing over homemade desserts or candy treats for the kids to enjoy.

Änna graduated high school and Carrie's parents had a huge graduation party at their farm shop. All the people Carrie grew up with and went to church with and all her family, friends, and relatives were there. My brother, Nabil brought my father, and my brother, Bassem came with his wife and son. It was a very special time for me and for our entire family. Carrie's friend and former co-worker from the law firm, Winifred, and Winifred's husband traveled to the graduation party, as well as Carrie's college friend, Valerie. Änna prepared to attend college at Carrie's alma mater. I knew it would take a miracle for the funding to go through, and God came through. At the last minute, she was able to attend. Änna was several hours away from us, but we were able to see her relatively frequently. She loved college and became very active there with work and studies. Änna likes to joke that she left for college and her replacement arrived.

In September, our second son arrived. I named him after my good friend, Sami. My father told Carrie after our son Sayf was born that, "insha allah, keman walid" or "if God wills, another son." He told Carrie that he was praying for another son for us, and his prayers were answered. Soon after Sami was born, he began turning blue and I had to run to the nurse's station because no one was responding to the alert button Carrie had pushed. Sami had fluid in his lungs, but was able to cough it out over time and did not have any serious repercussions from it. It happened that we had been placed in a room far from the main nurse's station. The nurse told us she assumed we would be experienced parents after five children and wouldn't need much assistance. Carrie was happy with her brood of children and being close to her parents. I was busy working, happy that she was happy.

The church Carrie and the children visited regularly was Living Word (yes –ANOTHER Living Word church). It turned out that Carrie knew two couples attending the church, as they had previously attended a church Carrie had often visited with her parents as a child.

I was not happy about Carrie attending church with the kids. I would allow her to take them for a while, and then I would get angry and she would not go, to appease me. Because the church was small, Carrie was able to talk several times with the pastor, John, and his wife, Kay. Carrie would tell me how nice they were. She would also attend intercessory prayer nights led by Kay and attended by up to three other women.

Carrie was surprised to learn from another congregation member that Kay was very ill with kidney disease. Carrie had no inkling, as Kay was always in church on Sunday, dressed beautifully, bubbly and kind to everyone, and visiting with people after church. Carrie learned that Pastor John and Kay lived on the same block as the house we were renting.

I had gotten upset with Carrie for attending church and she had not gone for some time. She had decided she needed to get part-time work outside the home, and had walked to her job interview at a clothing retailer. On the way there, she saw Pastor John come out of his house, along with his sons. They looked very sober. Carrie learned the next day that Kay had died and she had seen Pastor John and his family shortly after Kay's death.

Carrie asked me to attend Kay's wake, but I refused to do so. So Carrie attended with Änna. Carrie was very moved after attending. Soon after, we were sitting outside our garage and Pastor John passed by, walking the dog. Carrie called out to him and introduced him to me. He ended up staying and visiting for quite some time. He explained that the dog was not himself since Kay passed away, that the dog was inconsolable. He poured out his heart to me about the pain he was experiencing at the loss of his wife. I saw him again a time or two when he was out walking his dog.

Pastor John ended up taking a leave of absence from the church for six months. Carrie would attend off and on and the congregation kept holding on and praying that Pastor John would return. The church had to sell their van to make ends meet, and the congregants stepped up to the plate to reach out to others, preach, continue Wednesday services, and try to do all that was necessary to keep the church going.

Carrie was able to continue to work from home for the attorney in Illinois. We were able to purchase a home in July 2008. As we were a little short on the down payment, Carrie volunteered to sell some of her gold to contribute to the purchase of our home.

Throughout this time, Carrie's friend, Winifred continued to be a support to her through scheduled weekly visits by telephone and through faithful prayer. She would counsel Carrie and would diligently pray for the many issues that arose with me and the children. Carrie considered Winifred one of her closest friends.

In August 2008, Nabil's family arrived from Jordan. His asylum petition had been approved some time earlier, and his wife and four children were subsequently cleared to join him. I was very happy for my brother to have his family back with him. They were separated over five years – far too long. Our children are close to the same ages and it was great to see the cousins develop relationships with one another.

We started having a lot of difficulties with our daughter, Marina. She always struggled with making friends. When she started middle school, she made some poor choices. I always felt that I could relate to Marina, could understand how her thought processes worked, better than Carrie could. Carrie was far too trusting. Although Marina was struggling socially, she did well academically. We went to parent-teacher conferences and met Marina's teacher, Kristine. This teacher was very kind and supportive of Marina. We found out that she was the worship leader at Living Word — another church connection.

I was concerned that Marina was developing unhealthy patterns and I immediately decided to pull her from public middle school. I knew from Carrie that there was a Christian school nearby. I contacted the principal there to see whether Marina could attend because it was not even the middle of the school year yet. It turned out that the principal was the church pianist at Living Word. Yet another Living Word connection! I was very impressed with the principal and with the school, and Marina began attending there.

Carrie's mother, Shirley, had worked for some time for Signe, the state attorney in another county. Signe was a Christian woman with a gift for discerning truth. She was very good to Shirley and they would often pray over situations encountered in their office, as well as before she would have to argue in the courtroom. Signe was married to a farmer, Donald, who had a retail business that was open only during the winter months. As he had lots of shop work he needed to accomplish, Donald needed help in his store and I was offered the job. I worked weekends in my manufacturing position and weekdays at the retail store, which was over an hour from my home. However, I greatly appreciated this job as it helped us financially in paying for the extra expense of private Christian school for Marina. In addition, this couple had a daughter close to Aisha's age. They were wonderful to have Aisha spend time at their home and take her with them to Bible camps and on other excursions. Some of Aisha's happiest memories are her times spent with this family.

Pastor John made the decision to return to preaching and the church rejoiced that he had returned. He began visiting each family who had stayed with the church while he was gone, to reacquaint himself with people and to get to know them better. I agreed to have him over and Carrie prepared an Arabic meal. He spent quite some time afterwards visiting with us.

Pastor John was always very loving to our children and would spend time talking with them when he saw them. The children had become quite established in their church youth group and Sunday school classes. They had bonded with the youth leaders, their class-mates, and with Pastor John. Living Word was unique in that it had a Wednesday evening service as well as a Sunday morning service, and Carrie loved to attend the Wednesday services. Often, because of my frustration with her attending Sunday services, she found it easier to attend Wednesday nights, as I seemed to put up less resistance.

In March 2009, Carrie applied for and received a job as a case worker for a refugee resettlement program under the umbrella of a social services organization. She absolutely loved this job, saying it was the best job she ever had. She had been working part-time from home since 2006, so this was a big change. She threw herself into the job and, because her strength is mercy, she was pouring her heart and soul into the refugees and the program. In fact, she was working night and day (often refugees would arrive on the midnight flight) and weekends as well. She was hardly at home.

Because my production supervisor position was a three-day, weekend position, I would be home with the kids for four days. However, because Carrie wasn't home, the house fell apart, we were eating out much of the time, and everything became unbalanced. I became very jealous. Carrie would transport people to and from medical appointments, social service agencies, public housing, the grocery store, school, job training and more. She would set up apartments, pick up donations, and haul furniture. It was never ending. I would follow her around town, bring her coffee, and ask her why she was wearing a certain dress or skirt because I thought they were too short.

Carrie had a good friend and co-worker from the law firm she had worked at in the city. This friend, Heidi, had been confined to a wheelchair since the age of four, and had a companion dog. Our daughter Marina would sometimes dog-sit Heidi's dog. When the firm would have its holiday party, Carrie and I would often sit with Heidi and her boyfriend, Tim. Heidi and Tim even came to visit us when we lived in Missouri, as Heidi had relatives in Missouri as well.

Heidi and Tim became engaged, and Heidi asked Carrie to be a bridesmaid in her wedding. Carrie asked me for permission, and I told her this was fine. Later, Heidi called to notify Carrie of her bridesmaid dress selection. Carrie asked me for permission to order the dress. I told her to order the dress. Two weeks before the wedding, Carrie talked to me about the details surrounding the wedding and when she would have to leave for the city. I got very angry and told her that she was not allowed to go. Carrie actually stood up to me and said that she had to go as she could not back out on her friend two weeks before the wedding. In fact, Heidi's sister had backed out earlier. Carrie said she absolutely would not put Heidi through this again.

I was firm. If she would go through with participating in the wedding, I would leave her. It was the worst fight we had ever had. I finally decided to call Pastor John.

Carrie would always say that Pastor John taught that wives were to obey God first and then to honor their husbands. I was positive Pastor John would back me up on this. To my surprise, Pastor did not back me up on this and could see no problem with Carrie walking down the aisle with a groomsman. I do not know why I was so angry and jealous at this time, but this was the bottom line – I was insanely jealous.

Carrie traveled to the wedding. She stayed with Winifred and her husband, and was a nervous wreck the entire time. Apparently, she hardly ate or slept, as she didn't know if I would still be home when she returned. I left her many messages stating that I would leave her. I completely ruined the entire experience for her. When she arrived home, I left and stayed in a hotel for the night. While I told myself that I was going to leave her for good, I ultimately returned home, explaining that I was staying because of our children. I gave Carrie the silent treatment for weeks, and our marriage almost didn't survive. It was really bad for many months.

Dream Turned Nightmare

It had always been my dream to have my own business. My father had two different businesses, and my brother, Nabil, had two businesses in his city. I had started to buy and sell cars here and there, and two friends of mine from the city convinced me to open a used car dealership. These friends buy vehicles at auctions around the country for their employer in the Gulf, and then they ship the cars overseas where they are fixed inexpensively. According to the law in the state where I lived, the only way I could legally buy and sell cars would be to physically have an office. My friends convinced me to join their plan. They would supply the cars, I would sell them, and I would give them what they paid. I could keep anything made over the cost of the vehicle.

I created a business with the State, found a good location, leased the space, painted the interior and prepared it for opening. My wife had met a Christian man from Ecuador at a refugee-related meeting. She learned that he had started his own printing business. I contacted him and he created a logo, business cards, and signage for my new business. Rico would witness to me about Christ and he drove me crazy.

It is interesting that, for the most important decision of my life financially, I did not consult our Christian family friend, Agnes, who had advised me for years. Part of this may be that, deep down, I knew she would not support this. I had mentioned my dream to her in passing a year or so before, and she had not encouraged it in any way.

I was somewhat delayed in opening my business. This was due to all the translating and transporting I was doing for the Arabic-speaking refugee community. I was involved with the gritty details of their lives. This included their very specific needs, fears, and stress as they adapted to a completely new country and culture, issues of abuse, suicide attempts and more. It was emotionally exhausting, but I wanted to help and was happy to do so.

When I finally did open my business, in August 2009, many of the refugees would come to me and ask to work for me on the side. They either did not have a job yet or the job they had was not enough for their families to make ends meet. I had one man do mechanic work for me, as he had been a mechanic in the Middle East. I asked him to rotate tires on a car my wife was driving. Carrie picked the car up from the dealership. On the way home, driving on the highway, a wheel came completely off the car. It was a blessing that she was not in an accident or seriously hurt. After that experience, I no longer had this individual do any mechanic work for me.

Another refugee, who had been given a car by a local church, would come to my dealership to work on his car, clean it, change oil, paint it, and more. I learned that he was taking whole cases of oil from the dealership, as well as auto cleaning supplies and other items. However, I did not confront him, as I figured he needed these things more than I did and it would all work out.

I quickly learned that the cars my friends were supplying me needed major work. As a new business owner, I had to learn the balance between how many repairs to make so the vehicle worked well and when to stop so that I could make a profit on the sale.

To complicate matters further, after a couple of sales of these vehicles, it became apparent that my friends either were so careless with their paperwork that they had no idea where the titles were located, they had never had the titles in the first place, or they were deliberately withholding the titles from me.

I was able to get a floor plan. This is a form of financing where a lender provided me a line of credit that I would purchase vehicles with, and then I would pay the lender as the vehicles were sold. In addition to the cars I had been provided by my friends, I was able to purchase a few vehicles using the floor plan. The man I had worked for the previous winter provided me with some of his inventory as well, as he was planning to close his business. My sales were very slowly increasing, and I was gaining a reputation of being fair. However, as my wife says, I do things with my heart and not with my head, and this is not a positive quality in the business world.

A man from the Middle East drove my children's bus. He knew my children's names were Arabic and he would ask them where their father was from. My children told him and he gave them a business card and asked them to have me call him. He did this on several occasions, so I finally did so. I learned that he would buy and sell cars one or two at a time and he was in desperate straits. He did not have enough money for rent and needed a place to live. I allowed him to work for me and sell some of his own cars from the dealership. I invited him to live at my place of business until he could save enough money for an apartment. This man's best friend was a well-respected physician at the hospital and this gave him credibility.

Trusting this man was another mistake on my part. When customers would show interest in my vehicles, this man would direct them to his vehicles. If vehicles needed some repair work, he would lie and tell customers that the vehicles worked fine. He would charge people double fees for repair work. He treated customers so poorly that I ended up paying a lot of extra money to correct his devious actions, to regain their trust and not lose the reputation of my business. Eventually, I could no longer put up with this man's behavior, and I told him to leave. But a lot of damage had already been done.

I had many situations where people would purchase a vehicle, drive it for a week or a month or two months, and bring it back and say they did not want the vehicle anymore. I took quite a few vehicles back and returned people's money to them. Further, I had people come to me after several months and say they could not afford the payments.

About this time, the organization Carrie worked for asked if it could utilize some of my business space to store winter coats, boots, hats and mittens. The agency is required by the government to provide these items to every refugee upon arrival. As my business was located close to the airport, I gave my key to the case worker, who could then stop at the dealership after picking up new arrivals and outfit them with the necessary winter items they needed. Again, I was happy to do this.

There was a particular refugee family we had gone the extra mile for. Carrie had personally prepared their arrival meal instead of purchasing a meal, which was more typical. I provided them with a cell phone free of charge, as I had done for many refugee families. Soon after arriving, the wife became ill. The husband was struggling with English and needed work. I hired him to do various jobs around the dealership and paid him cash. One time, while visiting at their home, the wife asked to read our fortunes in the coffee grounds. We refused, but she made a point of letting us know that she is proficient in such things and more.

Another time, I was called to their home to mediate between them. One spouse accused the other spouse of abuse. Later, this couple decided to sell the car they had been gifted. I advertised their vehicle in a weekly auto magazine and paid for all advertising myself. They sold their car and kept the proceeds from the sale. I did not ask for or take any money from the sale of their car. They told me they would like to buy a vehicle from me but they did not like any of the vehicles on my lot. I gave them a vehicle to drive free of charge. They drove this vehicle and many different vehicles over a period of six months. They eventually purchased a vehicle, but came back to me after a few weeks to say that they did not like it and that they wanted another vehicle. I then took them with me to the auction. This couple hand-selected which vehicle they wanted. I paid $3,895 for this vehicle using my floor plan and this couple agreed to make monthly payments. They paid only $2,000 and then stopped paying. After driving this vehicle for some time, they decided they did not like this vehicle either. I then agreed to take the vehicle back to sell and they were to choose a vehicle on the lot in the $2,000 range. It was one thing after another.

There were also several situations where I had to repossess vehicles because people had not paid. I would give them a period of two months and up to four months to work with me before resorting to repossessing. Sometimes the vehicles would be in areas up to three hours away. I would have to notify law enforcement in those cities that I was repossessing a vehicle, in case the police would receive a call stating that a car had been stolen when, in fact, I had repossessed the car.

Even though business was gradually getting better, I was really struggling. I had never run a business before. Further, I was dealing with a lot of refugees from the Middle East and they asked a lot from me. I was a lifeline for them, in a sense, because I spoke Arabic and I had lived in the U.S. for many years. They relied on me to help them navigate around. Further, I felt a lot of pressure to assist them and would go above and beyond at the expense of my business, both with my time and financially. One of the first Middle Eastern refugees to arrive in the community became a very close friend of mine and still is. He would often go with me to assist other families. After a time, he completely withdrew from getting involved with the refugees due to all the infighting, jealousies and dislike between the various families and groups.

Additionally, my daughter, Änna had her heart set on studying abroad in Israel for a year. Her first year of college, she enrolled in a course about the Arab-Israeli conflict that was taught by an Israeli professor husband and wife team. This couple has become almost like second parents to Änna and has been a great encouragement and blessing to her. Änna planned to study in Jerusalem, taking both Arabic and Hebrew. Again, as Änna is very strong, she convinced me that her year abroad would actually be less expensive than living on campus and attending the university for a year. This turned out to not be the case. I received calls from her asking for food, money, or other assistance throughout her stay there. In addition, she became very lonesome right after Christmas and I ended up flying her home and back to Israel in the middle of the year – an extra flight expense we had not planned on.

A man named Roger came to look at a car in April 2010. We had a good visit, and he came back to see me again. He offered to help me in my business. It turns out his father was a dealer, his brothers had worked as car dealers, and he had even sold a popular state legislator his first vehicle. Cars were in Roger's blood.

Roger helped me immensely. He had gone back to school and was nearly finished with his bachelor's degree. His goal was to go on to law school. He has a legal mind, has been through a lot in his lifetime, and really knew the legal system and how the world worked. He taught me how to clinch a sale. He advised me on how to be a businessman and not all heart. He taught me sound business practices as he could see that I was not doing well. Because I was struggling financially, my friends told me that I should pay the floor planner first and then pay taxes as additional sales came in. I was getting further and further behind in registering cars. Roger told me that this was against the law and that I had to get it corrected as soon as possible. With Roger's advice, I contacted my attorney and set up a trustee account to pay taxes and register vehicles.

Over the summer, Sayf and Aisha took swimming lessons. Sayf had also signed up for basketball and really enjoyed it. Aisha enrolled in volleyball, partici- pated in the community youth choir, and played violin in the orchestra. Both Aisha and Sayf enjoyed play dates with their friends and loved to be at home – Aisha reading and Sayf playing with Sami in the back yard.

A parenting class was held at church. Carrie asked me to attend with her as we were struggling with var- ious behaviors with our children. I attended, along with a number of other parents, including two couples from Nigeria who were medical doctors. I could tell from attending this class that these parents loved God and were trying to raise their children to love and respect both God and others. I was very impressed with this. I could relate to some of the cultural issues the Nige- rians brought up. I was also very moved by various statements made by the American couples. I appreciated Pastor John's leadership in this class as well.

Not long after this, another local pastor came into the dealership with a young college student from Pakistan who attended his church. We ended up talking together for quite some time, and on more than one occasion in connection with the sale of a vehicle to the Pakistani young woman. At one point, she gave her testimony of leaving Islam and coming to Christ. I listened, but did not say much.

After a year-long courtship, Pastor John and Kristine, Marina's former teacher and the worship leader, were married. Carrie and I were invited to the reception and we attended together. I had gotten to know Pastor John, Kristine, and many of the people by this time through those I had met through the Christian school Marina attended, and through parenting classes at church.

Marina was now in high school and was struggling again. We believe she was fighting depression, as well as struggling with finding friends. She had made two relatively close friends, and then both these friends moved out of the area.

Carrie continued to attend church. I would allow it for a while, then forbid the children from going, then allow it again. Carrie was really struggling. Because I was working seven days a week, either as a production supervisor or at the dealership, and was working from 4 a.m. until 9 p.m., Carrie was responsible for all four children. She could not continue working as the children were simply left to themselves. It was not a healthy situation. After much agonizing, she made the decision to leave her job.

Shirley had been complaining for some time that she was more tired than usual and she appeared pale, with almost a grayish tone to her face. We were busy with our business and didn't think too much of it. However, it had been enough of an issue for us to comment that Shirley was not herself. We celebrated Thanksgiving and David and Shirley came, but she was not her usual bustling personality. A few days later, David called Carrie to tell her that Shirley had a temperature. Carrie advised him to get her to the doctor. He took her to the nurse-practitioner in their small hometown.

After a quick examination, the nurse-practitioner told David to get Shirley to the Emergency Room in the town we lived in, as this town had the largest clinic and hospital in the area. Shirley was admitted to ICU as the doctors determined she had a blood clot in her lung. Her recovery was long and we almost lost her. Because of the lack of oxygen, she struggled with memory loss.

David and Shirley lived on a farm near a river that frequently experienced major floods. They had experienced water in their basement a number of times, not due to the river flooding (as David had built a substantial dike around their home and shop) but rather from rainfall and water inside the dike getting into the basement. David had done some landscaping in an attempt to correct this, but the home was also in need of new windows and siding. Over time, the house had developed some mold. David would clean this mold, but he had experienced more water recently and had not had an opportunity to work on clean-up since that time.

Some years prior, David had been forced to stop farming because of all the losses he sustained from the many floods on this river. He found a job somewhat related to his education degree in that he was now working as an adaptive equipment specialist in a nearby town.

For the past several months and possibly the last couple years, both David and Shirley had not been feeling as well as they had in the past. David had always attributed this to the natural process of aging. However, after Shirley's health scare, David began to wonder if it could be related to mold.

Shirley's former boss, Signe, was now serving in another county. She called David to check on Shirley as Shirley was in the hospital for nearly a month. Because she owned town homes in the town where David worked, she suggested that he move Shirley there when released from the hospital, instead of back to the farm. David and Carrie discussed this and decided that it was a good idea as Shirley, in her weakened state, would not be able to take care of her large home on the farm until she was stronger and healthier. David purposed that this would be temporary, only until Shirley regained her health.

Max 1979 New House

Max 1985 Army

Max's Home City

Barhoum

Another Street in Max's Home City

Max's Childhood Home 1968 to 1979

Ajloun

Max Hunting 1988

Max and Friend

Max in Father's Store

Max's Father Cooking

Max's Father's Store

Front Entrance of Max's Parents' Home

Grapes in Front of Max's Parents' Home

Grandfather's Mosque in Jordan Valley

Max's Grandfather

Jordan Valley

Entrance to Max's High School

Max's High School Machine Shop

Sea of Galilee as Seen from Jordan

Petra

Änna and Uncle Bassem

Abdulrahim at the Airport 1992
After Seeing Carrie Off to the U.S.

Carrie in Israel 1986

Carrie's Parents

David and Änna 1989

Family Photo Christmas 2011

Family Photo Jordan 2002

Sayf and Aisha

Max and Carrie Day After Marriage at the Dead Sea

Newlyweds Max and Carrie at Tamara's Home

Salvation

C arrie was getting very weary. She had been praying for my salvation for years, and she was seriously considering divorce. While I had never been a liar, I was also not open with her about many things, especially finances. She did not trust me in this area at all. Now that I was running a business and never home, she felt isolated and even more mistrustful of me. Further, she had been praying for my salvation for eighteen years and, rather than things getting better, it looked like I was even more obstinate and firm in Islam. I was also more distant from her due to my preoccupation with business concerns and responsibilities. Our disagreements on religion were seemingly getting worse as the years went by.

Max's Family

Änna 1992

One Wednesday evening, a night when she had decided after much prayer that she was going to leave me, she attended church. The service was led by a Nigerian doctor's husband. He talked about the importance of God's appointed time and how God's appointed time is always the right time. This gave Carrie hope that I would come to salvation after all. She decided to delay moving forward with divorce. About this time, Aisha was given a solo part in the Christmas program, and Carrie asked me to attend, so I did.

The following January, my company laid off nearly 200 employees. I was one of them, as I was one of the highest paid production supervisors. In addition, I was seriously in trouble with my business. I had taken out a second mortgage on our home the previous July (against Carrie's wishes), and I was ready to close the doors.

I was laid off on Monday. My sister, Tamara, called me within an hour of the layoff. She seems to sense exactly when she needs to call and check on me. It happened that Pastor John was ushering in the 2011 New Year with a week of prayer. Each night was designated for a specific prayer topic; e.g., finances, healing, miracles, Israel, and our nation. Carrie had attended the first two nights and had shared with me about it. The third night, the night designated for miracles, Carrie asked me if I would please attend church with her because we were in desperate circumstances. I agreed to attend.

We drove separately because my dealership was just a little down the road from the church. We met at church and sat down. Pastor soon gave an invitation to come to the front if anyone needed a miracle. I could feel something pulling on my shoulder. I looked behind me. There was no one sitting directly behind me – but rather two rows behind me.

I looked at Carrie and said, "We need a miracle," so we got up and went to the front. I felt physically pushed from behind as I walked up the aisle.

Pastor looked at me and said, "I know you need a financial miracle, but the greatest miracle of all is salvation. Do you want to accept Christ?"

I said yes. With tears pouring down my face, I recited the sinner's prayer and invited Jesus into my heart. I was immediately flooded with a peace I had never known. After the service, Pastor gave me a

Bible. I was surrounded by people congratulating me and hugging me.

I left the church and got into my car. Carrie stopped by and asked me through the window, "Did you really just accept Christ?" I just smirked at her. She didn't know what to believe.

We got home. I went to sit in my chair in the living room. Before I realized what was happening, the dog was sitting next to me. Over time, I had gone from tolerating the dog to intensely disliking him, and the dog knew it. When he would hear the garage door opening at night, he would run to the basement and hide under the bed in the furthest room possible. He would not come out until I had left in the morning. The night I accepted Christ, Finn came and sat next to my chair in the living room. Carrie was shocked. Finn knew that I was a new creature in Christ because he actually sat next to me. This convinced Carrie that I had sincerely accepted Christ; it was the real deal. The dog now sleeps at my feet every night. It is amazing how perceptive animals are.

Carrie shared the exciting news about my salvation with her parents, Agnes, and her friend Winifred, as

Winifred had been praying for me and our family for many months and years. Winifred was thrilled with this news. However, because Carrie was so busy with work and the children, it was far more difficult to connect due to time constraints on Carrie's part.

Pastor John had given me *The Faith Aid* by Jim Kaseman, as our church was under the umbrella of his ministry. This aid contained faith confessions taken from the Bible. I began to recite them each day. There were a number of categories such as, "What I Am In Christ," "Where I Am In Christ," and more, and I would confess everything under every category on the faith aid. While spiritually I was coming alive, the rest of my life was falling apart. However, now I didn't have to rely on my wife's prayers and my in-laws' prayers – I could pray myself. Carrie and I prayed and asked God to help me find a new job, and we also prayed about the business. We made a practice of praying every morning together.

One of Carrie's friends from church had given her a book about the Holy Spirit. Carrie read the book. The author shared that receiving the gift of the Holy Spirit was as simple as praying and asking for it. Carrie was so happy that I had received Christ. She wanted me to experience all that the Lord has provided for believers. We were sitting on the sofa during one of our prayer times together. Carrie explained the gift of the Holy Spirit and asked if I wanted to receive this gift. I told her yes and we prayed together. I immediately began speaking in tongues. It felt weird to be speaking words that I didn't understand. Carrie explained that, when we don't know how to pray, if we pray in the Spirit, we pray God's heart in the matter.

Attack

I decided to sell everything from the business including tools, cars, furniture, auto supplies and more, pay as much debt as possible, and close the doors. The man who did all my business printing, Rico, recommended an auctioneer, Leif, and I contacted him. To my surprise, the auctioneer said, "Instead of selling everything, why don't I go into partnership with you?" I thought this was an answer to prayer. Also, it happened that Leif attended the church of the pastor who had come in with the Pakistani student. Leif made a point of saying to me, "The only reason I am willing to go into business with you is because you have become a Christian. If you were not a Christian, I could not be in partnership with you because we would be unequally yoked."I thought Leif was a sincere and devout Christian.

Roger and I met with Leif and another man who was considering entering the partnership as well. Carrie did not feel good about it. I called Pastor John and told him about Leif's offer. It seemed to me that this was an answer to prayer. Pastor John did not advocate for or against this partnership. Rather, he listened to me, as he had been a businessman prior to becoming a pastor. Leif's partner in his previous car dealership, Kenny, decided against entering into the partnership. We later learned that two families in our small church had been defrauded by Leif. But these families did not know I was partnering with Leif until the paperwork had already been signed. These families later expressed that, had they known who I had decided to partner with, they would have talked to me and advised that I reconsider such a partnership. But they simply didn't know as the partnership was established quickly and I only saw my church family on Sundays. If two families in our small church had been taken, then what about the greater community? While Pastor John may have heard about some of these situations, he is a man of integrity and will not speak ill of anyone. By Valentine's Day, I had signed all the necessary legal documents to make Leif my business partner.

Meanwhile, Carrie actively searched for jobs for me and the church actively prayed for me. I had three interviews and I was offered three jobs. I accepted a job with an agricultural equipment manufacturer in a town over an hour away. As part of the company's relocation package, they helped sell our home. We were blessed to find a buyer and we were able to sell our home by the end of April. I had started working at the new job in March and was commuting every day. I was totally out of the car dealership by the end of March.

Sami loved to be at home and to play at home. Because I was working long hours in another town, Carrie's parents helped her with the final chores related to moving from the house. Shirley often remarks on the following: When pulling out of the driveway, Sami let out a deep, heart wrenching sob that rose to a roar at leaving his beloved home. He frequently expresses, "I want to go back to our red house." In fact, he did so just today before I sat down to write this. The move from that house was very traumatic on our little Sami, and he has mourned the loss of that home ever since.

It had become apparent that I could not work at this new job and participate in the car dealership. It was decided that Leif would take over the entire business. I turned everything over to him, including the inventory from the man I had worked for in another town, with the idea that Leif would give the proceeds from the sale of these items to me and I would then pay this man accordingly. I moved to the new town in April. We continued attending church at Living Word. Pastor John held an immersion water baptism in April. Both Sayf and I were baptized. When I came up out of the water, I felt like I was washed totally clean and a new life was ahead of me.

I was making more money than I had ever made before at my new job. This was a huge blessing. I was able to pour most of my salary, other than living expenses and monthly bill obligations, into the taxes and title registrations that I had gotten behind in. I still had titles to nine cars and an additional four titles with the floor planner for a total of thirteen vehicles. I was receiving monthly payments for an additional five vehicles. The agreement was that any cars of mine which sold were to go to my car registrations and title obligations, and any cars Leif sold were to go into paying the lease, advertising expenses, etc. Roger stayed on with my partner to assist in a smooth transition.

It was not too long before I was hearing frightening things from Roger. Leif had been working with another man, Anthony, for years. Anthony assisted Leif with his auctions. Anthony was running the dealership business while Leif continued his auction and insurance businesses. Apparently, on the day that the business was formally acquired by Leif, he was walking around the dealership saying, "April Fool's on Max!" and laughing.

Roger learned that Leif lived in one state, but ran three businesses under other people's names, out of my state. He also learned that Leif was a high school buddy of a county official and that Leif ran annual fundraising auctions. Anthony told Roger that Leif was very smart and knew how to avoid getting pinned with any felonies by always keeping amounts below $5,000. Further, Leif would have Anthony sign almost all documentation so that he, Leif, could never be prosecuted.

In April, when Leif acquired full ownership, the agreement was to acquire assets of the dealership. A vehicle was on the lot for sale and the title was in the vehicle file. Leif had been told that this vehicle was a consignment vehicle and not part of the inventory. When informed that the vehicle had been sold and that a local bank held a lien on the vehicle, Leif's response was, "I have the title. I have the vehicle. It's mine. I'm selling it." The bank faxed a copy of the bill of sale and Leif reiterated, "I have the title. It's mine and I'm selling it."

Roger looked through the dealership for the original bill of sale, and after extensive searching finally found it buried underneath a file cabinet drawer where it had fallen. When approached by Roger again and told he couldn't sell the vehicle as the title had to be forwarded to the bank, Leif flat out refused and said, "It's mine. I'm selling it." In early June, Leif illegally sold the vehicle on in-house financing, knowing that the vehicle had a lien from a bank.

While doing business at the dealership, Leif made sure that any and all documents involving day-to-day operations did not have his signature. He used the signatures of Roger, Anthony and other employees to avoid having his signature on legal documents. This included bills of sale, license registration forms, titles, and temporary drive-out stickers. Leif would only sign when absolutely required. Anthony commented several times that this was Leif's modus operandi, "This is how Leif does it." Anthony confided to Roger that he and Leif had a long association and that even he (Anthony) had to scam Leif to get paid.

People started coming to the dealership and Roger would ask to assist them. They would say that they were not there to purchase a car. Rather, Leif had run their auction and, even though six months or a year had passed, Leif had never paid them for their items that had sold.

While working there, Roger witnessed at least two services of process where people were coming after Leif for unpaid monies related to prior auctions. Anthony told Roger that Leif had been served over thirty lawsuits related to his auction and other businesses. During another conversation, Anthony told Roger that Leif rigged his auctions. Leif used his auction company as a front to give himself a good name in the community as a benefactor to nonprofits. He provided his auction services to be used for fundraising with the appearance that he was donating his fee. Anthony told Roger that Leif skimmed money off the top by misreporting the actual selling price of items auctioned, and that Leif did this with all his auctions. Further, Anthony reciprocated and did the same thing in return back against Leif, to compensate himself for services to Leif.

Leif was a very smooth talker. He convinced Roger that he should have the titles for the "buy here, pay here" vehicles, and for the thirteen vehicles I left on the lot. Roger came to me and gave his word that, if I gave him the titles, he (Roger) would ensure that they were taken care of properly and left in the dealership. While I had a strong, inner feeling that I was not to hand the titles over, Roger finally convinced me to do so. Within days of my handing the titles to Roger, Leif had taken them home with him and would not return them.

Anthony came to Roger multiple times with files, knowing Roger had signatory on the account. Anthony asked Roger if he could go down and pay the sales tax and licenses on these files because the loan company was calling inquiring why the paperwork had not been done. Roger attempted, on three occasions between April and June 2011, to take files down to the DMV to register cars. He was unable to complete the registrations because Leif did not have the funds in the checking account after being paid by the finance company.

Things went downhill quickly after this. There were two situations where refugees had purchased cars from me, had returned their cars to me to purchase different vehicles, and Leif simply took the money and did not purchase vehicles for them. Leif also sold vehicles that were part of the floor plan and did not pay the floor planner at all. He did not make lease payments, telephone payments, mechanic payments or advertising payments for the business. He was not registering cars or titles, either.

Anthony told Roger that Leif had sold all of my contracts to a financial company for pennies on the dollar. He also informed Roger that Leif had been pulling this fraud with failing businesses for the last ten years, as well as defrauding the public. Anthony informed Roger that Leif would never have to be worried about legalities because Leif was personal friends with a county official.

One day, I received a call from my local bank. I personally knew the vice president as he went to high school with my wife. He told me three large dealership checks had come through and the signatures were clearly not mine. I had left everything at the dealership with complete trust in Leif, and it was now coming back to bite me in a major way. The vice president knew that I had turned the entire business over to Leif and he knew that I was working full-time in another city. If I had not been alert before, I was now keenly aware that there were serious issues going on.

To make matters worse, Leif sold cars that Roger had on the lot and did not give Roger any of the money. Then Leif did not pay the taxes or register the cars and let Roger take the fall. When Roger called the authorities to make a complaint, the officials said they would only take a complaint against me, not against Leif.

Roger said, "These are issues between me and Leif and have nothing to do with Mr. Tahtamouni."

The officials said, "We will only take complaints against Mr. Tahtamouni. We will not take any complaints against Leif."

Things were getting really bizarre. Roger and my attorney had been communicating regularly with the State Motor Vehicle Department in efforts to pay all outstanding taxes. Suddenly, all communication stopped. Roger learned that, while he was out of town, Leif had a meeting with the man from the State. Leif purposely planned the meeting during Roger's absence. Going forward, the State would not communicate at all with my attorney or with Roger.

Leif told Roger that he was going to close the business imminently. A customer came in and Leif sold the customer a warranty package. Leif told the customer to come in the following week to have a mechanical problem taken care of. When the customer left, Leif laughed about how the customer would come and be shocked to know that the doors were locked and the warranty was useless.

It was also interesting that Leif, as an insurance salesman (another method he used to defraud people by taking their insurance payments, pocketing the money instead of depositing it with the company, and then accusing people of not having paid the premium) had written his own bond for the dealership.

The next day, when Roger got to work, all the locks had been changed. Roger was officially out of the loop going forward. Who knew what Leif would pull next?

Roger wrote a letter to the State, with no response. So Roger drove to the capital to talk to the State official personally. When Roger confronted the man and asked him why he was illegally backdating paperwork to protect Leif, the man told him, "That is between me and Leif and none of your business." Roger also went to the Attorney General's office, where he learned that in our state, certain officials answer to no one. There is no one policing the police in this situation. Because of Roger rattling the cage in the capital, however, the head of one State agency lost his job.

Because Roger had learned how Leif ran illegal auctions, Roger began attending public auctions run by Leif. Roger would carry a clipboard and walk around looking at the sale items, just as other attendees were doing. Leif turned red and became very upset. He could soon be seen running outside and making frantic phone calls. Within a short while, a deputy walked up to Roger and told him that he had to leave the auction or he would be forcibly removed. Remember, this is a public auction, and Roger was doing nothing other than walking around, viewing sales items. This shows the level of power and corruption in the city – that a deputy would be discharged to an auction location to escort Roger from the sale at Leif's request.

In addition, Roger was harassed by law enforcement. They would drive by his home and follow him around town. One day he was in the north of town. An officer followed him all the way to the south of town, to the parking lot of a major retail store. Roger had been in two major car accidents and suffered damage to his nervous system. He suffers from vertigo and extreme pain and has handicapped driver plates. In this instance, Roger parked in the store's lot. The police stopped behind him diagonally and blocked him in the parking space. After some time, the officer backed up and left. I relayed this information to my attorney who was astounded at the level of intimidation that was taking place.

Roger also ran into Leif's previous car dealership partner, Kenny. This man told Roger that after they had dissolved their partnership, Leif had broken into his business, wiped his computer clean, and had stolen several cars. This resonated with Roger, because he had heard Leif bragging about doing just this to Kenny.

When I began learning about all the deception and craziness, I decided to get my personal items from the office, especially after the situation with the forged checks. Anthony was very menacing and I hardly got out with my personal paperwork and laptop, much less any of my tools or other items. Upon opening my laptop later at home, I learned that Leif had wiped my computer clean as well. Thankfully, all my business records were backed up with my accountant. Further, Leif took everything related to the business – all tools, furniture, auto parts and supplies, engine lifts, air compressors, pressure washer, kitchen cabinets, stove, refrigerator, dishes, room dividers, televisions, file cabinets, thirteen vehicles and the inventory Signe's husband had provided me when he decided to sell his business. Leif completely cleaned me out in every way. I am still paying the floor planner for the vehicles Leif sold and profited from that belonged to the floor planning company. Leif claimed to be a Christian, a follower of the Lord Jesus Christ. I forgive Leif and I ask God to bless him.

Former customers were calling me and telling me that they had received calls from a county official, asking them to file complaints against me. They told the official they had no complaints and asked why the official was calling them. Other people who had been taken by Leif went to file complaints and were told that complaints would only be accepted against me. When they said that they had no complaints against me because Leif was the one who had assisted them, the authorities told them they could not help them.

In May, Carrie received a message on Facebook from the wife of the refugee couple we had poured our hearts into. This woman demanded money from Carrie and made threats against Carrie's life and our children's lives. She said she would go to the media if she did not receive money from me. Carrie was sick to her stomach and overwrought. She remembered that this woman was into possible occult practices, and she was terrified of her and her threats.

My attorney learned that I was being investigated and that charges were coming down. He contacted the State Attorney's office nearly daily, and was told nothing. I told my employer that I had a dishonest business partner and that things were heating up related to taxes and other issues. My employer thanked me for being up front and told me to keep him informed.

Finally, when my attorney was on vacation, eighteen charges were handed down. They were eight felonies and ten misdemeanors. Most were related to car registrations and taxes. I had registered all my cars, and the charges against me were for cars that Leif had taken and had not paid. However, there was absolutely no investigation into my partner. I had been working to pay the taxes when all communication was cut, and again, this was related to Leif and the county officials' involvement.

I was told to turn myself in and that I would be given the opportunity to post bond. I called my brother Nabil and asked for financial assistance. Carrie had a small amount of gold left and sold nearly everything except her wedding ring and a pair of earrings so I could post bond. This aspect of Middle Eastern culture was God's provision in our time of need. While it is expensive to purchase gold initially, when times get difficult, gold can be sold and turned into cash if necessary. God miraculously provided for us in this way. The next day, my charges were on the front page of the city newspaper, the main paper for that region.

I received a call from my former neighbor around 5:30 or 6 a.m. He was very upset and asked if I had seen the morning paper. I told him no. He told me to locate a paper and read it as soon as possible. Later that day, he called me again with great concern, and he and his wife drove to our home in a town an hour away to check on us and to show support. The paper painted a terrible story of me as a Middle Eastern man who preyed on innocent refugees and Americans and defrauded them of their hard-earned money. It did not tell the whole story – did not even attempt to provide fair and honest reporting. It did not mention that I had a partner who took over my business. It did not report that this partner had over thirty lawsuits against him, whereas I had a clean record other than a few speeding tickets from many years before. The article quoted from the very refugees I had helped the most and who WERE defrauded (but by Leif, not by me) and by the county investigator. We later learned that Leif and the county investigator were allegedly close friends with the news-paper editor. In particular, the county investigator had been prominently featured in this newspaper several times before and loved publicity and accolades. While I had been contacted the evening before at work by someone from the local paper, I had declined to speak with this person, as my attorney was on vacation.

To continue, the refugees quoted in the article included the couple who voluntarily brought their vehicle back to the lot for me to sell when they decided not to pay the full amount of $3,895 because they no longer liked the vehicle. They had paid $2,000 of the $3,895. I paid them the $2,000 and Leif sold their vehicle and pocketed the money, as he was now in total control of the dealership. They then decided that they wanted the money from the sale of the vehicle, even though it wasn't theirs because they had never paid for it and the amount they had paid had been reimbursed. This couple was greedy and wanted to get as much money as they could, even if doing so dishonestly. They happened to live next to the investigating officer and they were close acquaintances of this officer. Because of the corruption on the part of the city and state officials, this couple was allowed to file charges against me instead of Leif, even though they had already been compensated and

I had documented proof of this compensation. Even after this woman threatened Carrie on Facebook, I continued to provide and pay for their cell phone until the time of the newspaper article. My attorney asked this couple to drop the charges as they had already been reimbursed. This couple refused to do so.

In addition, as an auto dealer I had to have a bond. When my business failed, debtors were able to petition the bond for their losses. I learned that this same couple petitioned the bond for an amount higher than the purchase price of the vehicle and collected on the bond. Ultimately this couple received triple of what they had actually paid towards the vehicle. They went to the media, destroyed my reputation, and made threats towards my wife and children. I forgive them and ask God to bless them.

The day after the newspaper article appeared, I had training at work. The following Monday, I received a call from my employer stating that I was terminated. I was not allowed to give an explanation. I was not even paid for three days of work. When I attempted to meet with the employer for an explanation, I was denied a meeting. Again, within the hour, my sister, Tamara, called me to check on me.

To say that Carrie was devastated is an under-statement. She sank into total and utter despair. She was inconsolable and spent hours each day weeping. Pastor John called her and talked with her. He told her, "Remember in the Bible where it says, 'No weapon formed against you will prosper,' it means no weapon formed against you will prosper NOW – not just at the end of the battle." This registered in Carrie's heart. However, she kept asking why this was happening and how could such persecution be possible. Pastor John told her, "Jesus was scorned and rejected and He was completely innocent. He walked through all that you are walking through and more." Carrie could say nothing to this. Jesus led a perfect life and she had led anything but a perfect life. Jesus had willingly suffered persecution, torture and death because of His love for all people. She began to really think about the depth of Jesus' love for her and for the world.

At the time, Carrie was doing a Kenneth Hagin study on prayer via Skype with three women from church. The leader (and also the former principal of the

Christian school) told Carrie, "When this is over, there is going to be a praiseworthy, Tahtamouni testimony." This also took root in Carrie's heart and she clung to this over the following grueling months.

Carrie now lost all contact with Winifred. One of the last times they had spoken on the phone, Carrie felt that there was condemnation towards me for what was happening. This was simply too painful for her to hear. While Winifred was likely voicing her true feelings and was motivated out of concern for Carrie, Carrie was trying to stay strong, survive this legal battle and be a support to me. She just couldn't handle this from her closest friend. Carrie has deep regret over the loss of this friendship, particularly as Winifred had a recent battle with cancer and had needed Carrie's support when Carrie was least able to provide it. Until now, Carrie has not spoken with Winifred and this grieves her.

I now had no income, as I was fired from the best paying job I had ever had, which was allowing me to pay back the taxes. My attorney told me, "I know that you are a man of your word, so I'm assigning my litigator to your case and you can pay me back in the future when you have gotten through this mess." I was immediately seeing God's favor over my life, even in the midst of terrible circumstances.

First, God had provided Roger to stay on with Leif. Roger personally witnessed what was going on and witnessed first-hand that Leif was not a man of integrity or honesty. If Roger had not stayed on to work with Leif, I would not have known the level and depth of corruption taking place at the dealership under Leif's direction.

Second, God provided me with a new job that handled the sale of my house, which freed me completely from that city.

Third, this job had so much overtime that I was able to pay down much of the taxes and title registrations that I owed.

Fourth, my attorney stated he would represent me even though he would not get paid for quite some time, especially if I did jail time. This is unheard of! I don't know of many attorneys who work without being paid on time, and often they require money up front. This was miraculous!

At my first court appearance, Pastor John, Roger and Carrie attended with me. When my attorney asked the investigating officer why he had not contacted me, the officer said that he did not know where to find me. This was a total and absolute lie. My attorney personally knows this officer and he and this officer had talked, on at least two occasions, about the fact that this attorney was representing me. Further, my attorney had purposely gone to the place of business where this officer would go when getting off duty in order to ask what progress was being made on the investigation. So the officer lied outright on the stand. When my attorney showed the officer copies of the forged checks (where the fraudulent signatures were clearly not mine) that were written out after Leif took sole ownership of the business, the officer would not comment.

It was a very solemn moment when the charges were read out. Afterwards, looking very grave, Pastor John said, "You are going to need a miracle."

Carrie did not go to another court appearance. She simply could not handle it. Roger and David, however, came to each and every one. They stood by me one hundred percent at all times. My former neighbor also faithfully stood by me, as well as my brothers, who would call me frequently and check on me.

My attorney told me that he had never seen such corruption from the city level all the way to the state level, based on many situations they encountered with my case going forward. This was particularly difficult for Carrie because she grew up in that area, had Christian parents, and worked in the legal profession. She has always been passionate about justice and has obeyed the law to a tee. She taught our children to respect police officers, to obey the law, to always pay their bills, to return money if given incorrect change, and on and on. For her to see that there is corruption, deceit, and willful manipulation of the truth by county officials, individuals in law enforcement, and the justice system shook her to her very foundations.

In addition, the refugee woman's threatening e-mail came true in nearly every way: she went to the media, she caused me to lose more than one job, and she contributed to the destruction of our reputation. Carrie printed this woman's Facebook message and provided it to the attorney as evidence. However, because the case did not go to trial, this evidence was never made public. Carrie felt that the devil himself had won.

Carrie would spend up to two hours or more praying. She would audibly speak out Bible verses pertaining to wisdom, justice and mercy. She would confess that the truth would be revealed, that God's justice would reign, and more. Then she would collapse in tears and go to her closet where she would literally moan with grief. She thought that the family would be less likely to hear her if she was in her closet, not realizing that the closet backed up to the kitchen so we could probably hear her more clearly in her closet than if she had cried in her room.

Carrie would also pour out her heart to God. She would pray and say, "Thank you, Lord. You love us so much. You are correcting us because you correct those whom you love. We receive your correction."

Carrie had spoken to her mother's former boss, Signe, on several occasions. The first time Carrie called her, Carrie was very angry at me as she was still processing all that had happened. Signe did not comment too much at the time, but rather let Carrie talk. In subsequent conversations, after Carrie had reviewed all the documentation I provided and knew that I was telling the truth, she sensed that Signe did not seem to believe that I was innocent. This bothered Carrie terribly. Signe pointed out that I had broken the law by not paying the taxes and that the law was black and white, one either obeyed the law or did not. Carrie understood what Signe was saying, but also knew that the reason I had not paid the taxes was because I didn't have the money to do so. I had set up the trustee account with my attorney to ensure payment of the taxes; I had never intended to walk away from my financial obligations. I take full responsibility for my poor decisions. However, when Carrie told Signe all the crazy things that were going on with my former partner and the apparent support he was receiving from county officials and law enforcement, Signe told Carrie that she preferred not to believe that these officials could be corrupt in any way and that, whatever the truth was, it would come out.

Signe went on to say that it is human nature to protect oneself and one's family and to deny or excuse one's failures or sins. While Carrie understood this and had seen it throughout her lifetime in herself and in others, she also knew me before Christ and after I had received Christ. She knew in her heart that I was innocent of the charges I was being accused of. After receiving Christ, there was an immediate change in my heart and anything against what Christ or the Bible taught, I knew I could not support in any way, shape, or form. Carrie was seeing this in me. If she had doubts about my innocence before, she now gave me her complete and whole-hearted support.

I also called Signe several times and she kindly called me back. She was not ever mean or unkind to me. In fact, she and her husband had been nothing but wonderful to me and my family, inviting us to their home, welcoming our daughter Aisha, and more. Carrie's thought was, Signe is a Christian and it is up to the Lord to reveal Muhannad's innocence to her.

Soon after, Signe was of great help to me. One of my former customers had not made a vehicle payment for over six months. I called Signe, as this former customer lived in Signe's jurisdiction. I asked Signe if it was okay to repossess the vehicle. Signe told me that it should be fine, that I should call the police in that county, and proceed with the repossession. I called the authorities and left a copy of the bill of sale with the sheriff's department. A deputy accompanied me to the former customer's residence in case there would be any complications or anger on the part of the person I repossessed the vehicle from. I took the vehicle without incident and returned to my home over one hundred miles away. I placed the vehicle on a friend's car lot with the intention of selling it, unless the former customer should pay what she currently owed.

Six weeks later, I received a phone call from law enforcement in the county where I was currently residing, asking me to return the vehicle immediately or face arrest due to theft of property. I told the officer that the vehicle was mine and that I would not be returning it. I later learned that this officer had talked to an official in the county where I was charged. This officer was told that I had no right to repossess this vehicle, even if the lady had not made any payments. Essentially, the county official in the jurisdiction where I was charged wanted the woman to get this vehicle for free rather than support my legal right to repossess it. I told the officer that if the woman would pay the bank all that was owed on the vehicle, I would return the vehicle to her. This woman went to the dealership and talked to Leif. Leif told her that she did not need to pay me, that he would get the vehicle back for her. In fact, Leif had tried to take this vehicle himself in the past. He had not been able to do so as I was the lien holder. Because this vehicle was bundled with another loan through a bank, the woman had to pay the bank directly, not the dealership.

Leif went to this bank and demanded information from the bank officer. The bank officer called me and asked me what was going on. The bank officer knew I had repossessed the vehicle because I had alerted him prior to doing so. Because this woman had not made payments and because I was the lien holder, I had made two payments to the bank so that I could keep the vehicle until this woman came forth with the money she owed. The bank officer would not release information to Leif. The bank officer then received a visit from the investigating officer, who pressured him to release information that would allow the county offi-cial access to the paperwork. The bank officer gave in to this intimidation and complied with the investigating officer's request. I have a letter from this bank officer stating that his action was a violation of banking law and that he would agree to be a witness on my behalf should my case go to trial. Because of mismanagement on the part of the bank official when he released this information, the county official was able to request a new title and take possession of the vehicle. The vehicle was subsequently delivered to the woman. She paid the remainder of what was owed to the bank, minus the payments I had made. She did not pay the full amount, as I had made payments to the bank when this woman had neglected to do so. I had no voice and no right to protest this injustice regarding a vehicle that I legally owned, due to the corruption on the part of the county officials. They deliberately targeted me, harassed and intimidated my bank officer, and aided a woman who had defaulted on her loan obligations.

At the advice and assistance of the officials in the county where I was charged, this woman then filed charges against me for repossessing the vehicle that I owned. My attorney was able to get this charge dropped because it was absolutely ludicrous. I do not share this information to try to portray myself in a good light. I made many business errors and mistakes that were only corrected after Roger started assisting me and instructing me on proper protocol. Rather, I share this information to show that, while I had not been wise in my business, I was targeted as a scapegoat, either for Leif and his involvement with the county official, or because it would be a feather in the official's cap should a Middle Eastern man be brought down in his county.

I spent my time reading the Bible and trying to stay in faith. My unemployment was not sufficient to cover our living expenses or bills. It became apparent we would need to seek food assistance. Carrie cried and cried. When I told the case worker how hard it was for my wife to accept help, she called in an order to a food pantry to get us by until we could receive food assistance. When I picked up the food, there was a flower in with the edible items. Carrie was touched, as she loves flowers. This was a sign to her that God really cares, right down to the minutest detail.

Pastor John came to visit us on more than one occasion. He continued to offer love and encouragement. He spent time visiting with us in our home and he took us out to eat so we could get a change of scenery. He prayed with us and for us.

Before I was a Christian, I had fought Carrie on tithing. She would say that God commands Christians to give 10 percent. I thought this was crazy! In Islam, people only have to give 3 percent. I would always tell her to tithe on her money if she wanted, but I was not tithing on my income. But after becoming a Christian, it was clear to me that I was to tithe 10 percent, and I did so. After being fired, Carrie and I watched a lot of Pat Robertson's 700 Club programs. One day they interviewed a couple who tithed even on their unemployment. This couple had been amazingly blessed. We also tithed on our unemployment. We were greatly encouraged by this program.

In addition, assistance came from unexpected people. Carrie had gone to high school with a woman who happened to be working in the court system in the city where I was charged. Prior to things getting really bad for me at my business, this woman's son and our son, Sayf, had become good friends. After the newspaper article came out, this woman called Carrie and just let Carrie talk. She made no judgments, made little comment, just listened. Soon after, she came to visit Carrie and gave her a beautiful flower. She stayed to visit for several hours, allowing the boys to play. She continued to keep in touch with Carrie throughout the entire process. Carrie will never forget this woman's kindness.

Carrie learned from this situation how important it is not to judge. One never knows what goes on in another person's heart. While Carrie had always liked this woman in high school and had respected this woman's athletic prowess, she had always felt out of this woman's league as this woman moved in the popular crowd and was always busy with cheerleading and sports. Carrie had seen her on occasion at past school reunions or at church celebrations in their hometown, but they had only said hello and that is it. Yet when Carrie was in the middle of this ordeal, it was this woman who stood by her side from the beginning to the end, with great kindness and compassion. Carrie was overwhelmed and touched by this woman's acts of friendship that literally lifted her up when she was at her lowest.

Further, this woman gifted Sayf with her son's outgrown clothing, coats, boots, and sports-related items. We were not in a position to buy clothes for the kids at this time. She outfitted Sayf with more clothing than he had ever had in his lifetime! God really does care about people and their every need. All that is required is that they turn to Him, talk to Him, and ask. It is that simple!

Another close friend, whom Carrie had met at church and who was one of the first to purchase a vehicle from me, brought bags of her daughter's outgrown clothing for Aisha. This friend's daughter has great fashion sense and Aisha was thrilled to get these clothes. It was like Christmas every time more bags were delivered. In this way, God provided for both Sayf and Aisha's clothing needs when I was without work.

A close friend of Shirley's in the past, a woman who had taught Carrie how to play organ, had served as a Sunday school teacher at her local church and as a 4-H leader, whose family was close family friends throughout Carrie's childhood and young adulthood, sent us two very generous gifts. These gifts arrived at times when we were in desperate straits, were praying and trusting God for provision, but had no earthly idea as to where the funds would come from. We are so thankful to this family for their generosity and for their obedience when God prompted them to bless us. This must have been hard for them, because they had walked with Shirley through Carrie's pregnancy and subsequent marriage to a Muslim Arab. Yet they walked in love and kindness, even though they did not support Carrie's life decisions.

This woman's daughter sent Carrie cards of encouragement nearly every week. The cards would typically arrive on days that Carrie was struggling the most. This was not a coincidence. Carrie was grateful for each encouraging word that arrived from this woman.

We also received a beautiful letter of support from Carrie's grandmother Erma's son-in-law. This letter touched us and encouraged us greatly. David's youngest sister also wrote a kind letter of support to us and included a photocopy of a hymn that had been dear to her mother before she died. God was continually encouraging us and moving on our behalf, even when we were going through much pain and uncertainty due to my pending legal issues.

Immediately after being fired from the agricultural equipment manufacturing company, I actively searched for work throughout the United States. Carrie and I were also watching every *It's Supernatural* program.

We watched the program featuring an interview with Surprise Sithole. Surprise said, "An angel of the Lord is going to free some people in some things! There are some people, a man and his wife, who have been having a tremendous time – not a good time, not an excitement time – and they really need the freedom right now. I see a draining rainbow on them right now. They are sitting on the cushion, a brown cushion. God wants to touch them right now and release the major freedom – a blessing of releasing and freedom right now!"

Carrie and I looked at each other and said, "He's talking about us!" We were sitting on a dark brown sofa and behind us, in the kitchen, there was a rainbow colored curtain. We immediately grabbed hold of that word and claimed it for our own. Mr. Sithole had a heavy accent and we had some difficulty understanding him. In particular, we did not necessarily understand what a "draining rainbow" was, but we knew we had a rainbow curtain, and that was enough!

The programs that kept us in faith, encouraged us, and sustained us through these dark days included *It's Supernatural* with Sid Roth, *The 700 Club*, Jesse

Duplantis Ministries, Marilyn Hickey, and Jerry Savelle. We knew in our heads and our hearts that God was with us, so who could stand against us? But it was a heavy, heavy time and very easy to dwell on the circumstances instead of God's promises to us.

Carrie's father watched Dennis Jernigan interviewed on *It's Supernatural,* and called to tell me and Carrie to make sure to watch it. As we recorded all the programs, we quickly found it and viewed it. Carrie's dad ordered the CDs for himself and for us. Dennis' music ministered to us greatly. Carrie would listen to his CDs twenty-four/seven and completely wore out the CD with, "It's Gonna Be Alright Child."

Carrie sent an e-mail to Dennis, pouring her heart out about our situation. In response his son-in-law and booking agent, Kristopher, called us. We have developed a friendship with Kristopher, and hope to visit him and Dennis some time. Carrie's dad had hoped to bring Dennis to Living Word, but the timing has not worked out and Pastor John did not feel released to do so. We are still hopeful that this will take place – but now we are believing for our Wisconsin church to host him.

I received a job offer from a company in another state in early December. Carrie was less than thrilled, as she did not want to move there. We had recently watched Matt Sorger interviewed on *It's Supernatural,* and when Carrie went online to look up churches in that town, it happened that Matt was scheduled to speak at a church there. This was confirmation to Carrie that I should take this job, and so I did.

I told my employer that I was involved in a legal battle with a former business partner involving taxes. Again, my employer thanked me for being up front and told me to keep him informed. I was to start the week after Christmas.

The company paid for me to stay in a hotel. I would drive there on Monday, work until Saturday afternoon, and then spend Saturday evening through Monday morning with my family. We were thankful for my job, but the legal situation was hanging over our heads.

Our Living Word church family was so supportive during this time. We continued to drive there on Sundays to attend church. Different families gave us gas money to get to church and they provided our family with a beautiful Christmas. Many individuals and families would hand us an envelope with a gas card or cash or restaurant cards. A doctor's family blessed us with a generous gift, exactly when a major bill was due. Another family who had stood by us through everything, the same family who had provided clothing for Aisha, gave us a generous gift that helped pay for several pressing needs. They would faithfully visit us and would call us and check on us. They are still dear friends today. Other church members came to the town we were living in for business or medical purposes, but then met Carrie and took her out to eat. These same people had gifted us with gas and food money. God was so good to us and took care of our family's every need. One morning we woke up very late – at 9:20 a.m. – and church started at 10:00 a.m. We were in the car by about 9:35. I drove the speed limit all the way. We arrived at church right when praise and worship started. This was miraculous as we traveled over eighty miles in less than thirty minutes.

One weekend, when Roger and his wife were visiting us, we discussed my name and how it and my reputation were in ruins, utterly destroyed. Roger told me that I needed a new name. As we sat and visited, I thought about the changes in me since accepting Christ, how I was truly a changed person from the inside out. Roger was telling me that my new name needed to be strong, with a powerful and positive meaning. Roger then said, "I think you should be called Max." Carrie looked it up. Max means *greatest*. We all agreed this was a suitable name – not because I am the greatest, but because Christ is greatest and I was now in Christ. I called David and Shirley and let those close to me know that I was to be called Max going forward. Carrie, however, still prefers to call me Muhannad.

Soon after moving to this new town, Carrie contacted the Christian pregnancy counselor who had helped her many years before, as this counselor lived in the town we moved to. Carrie went to visit her and shared with her what we were going through. The counselor then shared her legal story – a story not ours to tell, other than that her center was viciously attacked by an official who supported abortion. All the counselor's assets were seized, and terrible accusations were made about her and her family. It went to trial and the first judge assigned to the case, a judge sympathetic to Christian values, died in a tragic accident just prior to the trial beginning. The next assigned judge was so disrespectful and demeaning that he would cuss and swear at the counselor during court and then remove this verbal abuse from the written record. She told Carrie stories that paled in comparison to what we were going through. This woman's case eventually went to the State Supreme Court and Pat Robertson's Regent University stepped in to assist, free of charge, as the outcome could affect Christians nationwide. The counselor won, but not until she had gone through years of pain, financial loss, and had her reputation destroyed. In fact, even her pastor and members of her congregation did not support her, yet she continued to attend the same church despite the treatment she received there.

This story, while very painful to hear, made Carrie realize that corruption and evil occurs in many places; we were not the only victims of corrupt officials in the legal system of our state. Carrie could see the pain still etched in the counselor's face, yet the counselor had chosen to forgive and to move on and to rebuild.

This counselor later offered Carrie part-time work in one of her businesses. She even allowed Carrie to bring Sami with her as I was out of town and we literally could not pay for daycare. In addition, she offered to hire Marina. This was Marina's first job outside the home. She literally blossomed while working at this store. The women who worked there were beautiful, Christian people who encouraged Carrie, doted on Marina, and made a huge difference in helping them both heal.

On January 18, 2012, I received a word from the father of David's pastor. He said that I will see Leif face-to-face one day and forgive him. He told me that there will be public vindication of my innocence, and that I will minister to Leif. This word has not been fulfilled yet.

On the legal front, I had gathered all my documentation. I had written proof of my innocence on all charges except two related to non-payment of taxes. I was guilty of not paying taxes, but had never intended to *not* pay the taxes. I had immediately set up a trustee account with my attorney. My attorney had been working with the State to pay everything off, up until Leif met with the State and all communication was cut off. All other charges directly or indirectly related to Leif and his actions after partnering with me and eventually taking over my business.

My attorney told Carrie that Leif was a career criminal who attacked failing businesses. He would take everything he could from these businesses and then pin blame on the former owner. We learned that one of the families at church had a son who was close friends with Leif. Leif, with his smooth talk, had defrauded our friend and convinced our friend's son that he, Leif, was innocent. Our friend's son turned on his own father! This is how good Leif is at deceiving others.

We learned from another woman that Leif's wife had told her that Leif bragged about his intention to take all he could and then pin the guilt on me. We also learned that the investigating officer had been heard by a number of people we know. He had been bragging in the bar about how he and the county official involved were going to take me down in a big way, and how it was going to bring fame and promotion to them as a result. By the time we learned of Leif's character and the many people he had left in his destructive path, we had already moved from that town and we were in the midst of fighting for financial and legal survival. Also, there was a definite sense from former victims that there was no legal recourse against Leif, as he had the law on his side through his friendships with officials in authority. Further, because of this man's smooth talking and movement with well-known business figures in the community, many people felt they would not be believed.

I had been offered two different plea agreements. I refused them both because they were absolutely ludicrous. I did not believe that God wanted me to accept responsibility for crimes I had not committed.

The timing of my court dates was interesting as well. One court date was on the anniversary of my salvation. The other court date was on Purim, when the Jews were saved from evil Haman. Again, God was in every detail of my situation and circumstances.

David and Shirley were wonderful to come visit us and to encourage us as much as possible. Marina had gradually made a few acquaintances. Aisha, due to her happy and social nature, had made solid, new friends. Sayf had done so as well. Sami was at home enjoying his childhood by playing and roughhousing.

God's provision could also be seen with Carrie's legal work. Whenever things were getting unbearably tight, the attorney would call and offer her one or more new cases. God's timing was and is impeccable. While Carrie's legal work is very detailed and intense, it would help her get her focus off her problems and thus helped get her through the long hours of wondering, "What is going to happen to our family?"

I believe that God took me to another state to protect me, in part from Carrie and Roger. Carrie was angry, hurt, and heartbroken. She was trying to stand in faith, but she was hardly holding it together. She would confess the Word for two hours and cry for four hours. She had victory one moment and total defeat the next. Roger, while well-intentioned, would drive down to visit me nearly every weekend and would speak the negative. He was not purposely trying to discourage me; he was just being *realistic*. I knew that I had to be in total faith. I could not listen to anyone say anything that was contrary to what I was believing God for. I was believing for God's justice, for the truth to come out, for no prison time, no work release, no ankle bracelet, no parole. I wasn't asking for much!

One day before work, I was in my hotel room. I received a call from my attorney regarding an additional and unwarranted charge against me. I sold a vehicle to a man and he was to pay the tax and registration fees directly to the DMV. Instead, when he learned of my legal troubles, he went to the authorities and filed charges against me, stating that I had neglected to pay the required fees. Thankfully, I had the purchase agreement showing that this man was responsible for these fees and my attorney was able to have the charge dropped.

Three additional people tried to pull the same thing. I was so discouraged and frustrated at these attacks and was breaking down emotionally from the continuous harassment and absurdity of what was taking place. My attorney called these charges *pathetic*. I started yelling at God, "I used to be a Muslim. I became a Christian. I thought You were going to support me and help me. I don't see Your support and I don't know if I should believe in You or trust You anymore. I'm sick and tired of all religion! If You even exist, show me that You care. Show me Yourself so I know that You exist." Then I laid face-down on the bed and cried. After a few minutes, I apologized to the Lord for my anger and lack of trust. After that, I fell asleep as I was exhausted.

When not at work, I spent my time away from my family praying and reading the Bible in my hotel room. My attorney called me and told me that a final plea agreement had been offered. My attorney e-mailed it to Carrie. She was devastated yet again. She was adamant that I could not accept this agreement because it meant I would accept responsibility for two felony charges and carried the possibility of up to six months in jail. I had not committed those crimes. More accurately, I had committed crimes by not paying timely taxes but had never intended *not* to pay the taxes. It was always my intent to pay them and all my actions clearly showed this. The remaining tax amount owed was $6,200. Ironically, Carrie was far more defensive of me than I was of myself.

Carrie knows how important it is to forgive others so that God can forgive us. We had gone through some very difficult situations with my family, earlier in our marriage. Carrie had been controlled by anger and bitterness towards them. She had heard R.T. Kendall interviewed on *Focus on the Family* one day. His book, *Total Forgiveness,* set her free. She had often preached to me about this prior to my becoming a Christian. To be fair, I had seen a total change of heart in her after reading the book.

At any rate, from day one, I completely forgave Leif, the refugees who lied about us, the investigating officer, the county officials, the newspaper reporter, my former employer, and everyone else involved. I purposed to do this, and I prayed blessings over these people. Carrie also did this. While God miraculously and instantly released me from holding on to any unforgiveness, for Carrie, it was a very purposeful and concentrated effort and sometimes a minute-by-minute decision.

I prayed about the final plea and did not feel comfortable taking it. I was perfectly at peace with going to a jury trial as I had all the documentation and paper trail to back up my story. My attorney, however, warned me that a fair trial would be impossible due to the corruption in the city and county. He relayed that the case was very complicated due to the many parties involved and that it would be difficult to bring clarity to the situation because of this. He brought up the fact that the citizens of that area are not known for their open minds or acceptance of foreigners. He thought it would be hard to find an unbiased jury. He pointed out that, if I was convicted, I was facing many years in prison. I told him I would think about it some more and get back to him.

My attorney advised me to contact an agency nearby that provided ankle bracelets in order to show good faith and that I was acting responsibly. I took the information from him and contacted the company. I audibly confessed, "I will not be wearing any ankle bracelets or be on work release." The company representative thanked me for contacting him and told me that he could do nothing until a sentence had been handed down.

I later received a call from my attorney stating that he had talked to the attorney for the State. This attorney told my attorney that, if I didn't take the plea, he would go for blood and maximum prison time. However, if I would take the plea, he would not argue for any jail time and would not contest anything my attorney requested from the judge.

Carrie, while literally livid with the injustice of the justice system, and still adamant about my innocence and the importance of fighting the good fight all the way to the end, eventually relented and told me to do what

I thought was right. Not only would I likely do minimal jail time with the plea, I would also save the family from a long, drawn-out trial and more public humiliation. She just couldn't believe that it was God's best for me to take this plea, but she released me to make my own decision.

So I prayed some more, but I did not feel released from the Lord to take the plea until half an hour before appearing in court. One of the main verses Carrie stood on throughout this time was Colossians 2:14, "having canceled the charge of our legal indebtedness, which stood against us and condemned us; he has taken it away, nailing it to the cross" (NIV).

There was still tax money owed. My father-in-law graciously provided this to me. Thus I was able to pay full restitution, $6,200, prior to sentencing. This was another miracle. Again, I cannot thank God enough for providing these funds to David and for his kindness and mercy in offering these funds to me. David stood by me in word and in deed throughout the entire nightmare. He stood in faith, trusting God for a good outcome.

This last court appearance for sentencing before the judge was on Purim, and God was faithful in a mighty way. I was convicted of two felony charges, which would change to misdemeanors after serving two years probation. The judge did not sentence me to any prison time and she did not ask that I wear an ankle bracelet or be on work release. I was praising God for His mercy. Carrie was thankful, but could not get over the thought, "I'm married to a convicted felon." She was still bitter in her heart and in a lot of pain.

I was told to visit the local parole officer. I was told to ask whether I was under that jurisdiction or another city's, and to work through whether I would be allowed to leave the state to work. Carrie went with me. When we got to the office, the parole officer there curled her lip at me, berated me, and said that it was not likely I could keep my out-of-state job. Then she abruptly told me to go to the parole officer in the town where I lived. It was humiliating, and Carrie took it very hard.

We drove over a hundred miles to our town and walked into the parole office. We were greeted by a smiling and kind woman who introduced us to the head parole officer. She was cordial and respectful. She immediately gave me written authorization to travel out-of-state for work. She told me that she would notify the office in the state where I worked, but she thought she could likely remain my parole officer because my home address was local. She said that, because it was business related and because I had already paid res- titution, she did not know why I was even on probation in the first place. She also said the other state would not likely bother with me because there was nothing to monitor.

When we left the parole officer's office, I told Carrie, "I will be released from parole in less than a year." She just looked at me and did not say anything.

The next day, I returned to work. I was so thankful that there had not been another newspaper article. But I was mistaken, because there *was* another newspaper article and it was just as venomous, possibly even more venomous, than the first. It even called into question the judge's decision, essentially reporting that I had gotten away with my crime and that true justice had not prevailed. The following day, I audibly heard Jesus speak to me. He said, "Pack everything." I also had a strong sense of urgency; that it had to be done prior to going to work. I knew that I was to completely pack up my belongings from the hotel room and get the entire printout of the charges for my stay there, prior to going to work. I walked into work, and after a short time, was called to the office. I could see the newspaper from my own town, the same newspaper that printed the biased and unbalanced story about me, on the HR person's desk. I was fired and told not to come back. I later learned that someone had hand-delivered the paper to my employer – a nearly four-hour drive. That is how deep the hatred ran in this situation. For the third time, my sister, Tamara, called from Jordan within an hour of my termination. She had sensed that something was wrong and she needed to talk to me.

As I was leaving that state, I heard, "Don't look back. I have good for you." I felt like Lot and his wife. I forced myself to laugh out loud at the devil as I drove home.

The minute I walked in the door, Carrie looked at me and said, "You were fired again!" She then ran to our room and cried. I could see God's hand in the situation again, however. I had found a home to lease near my job and had been ready to sign the paperwork. The company had provided the down payment. I was literally on my way to the leasing agent to sign when I received a call that the home had been sold and was no longer available. The agent told me that the home had been on the market for many months. The buyer had materialized out of nowhere and was in a position to buy immediately. If that down payment check had been cashed, I would have owed the company that money, would have been locked into a lease that I could not pay because I did not have a job, and it would have been a bad situation.

I soon learned that the company refused to pay unemployment and planned to charge me for my hotel stay from December through March. I located another attorney, at the request of my main attorney, who does not deal with employment termination issues. One call from the new attorney to my previous employer put a stop to the employer's request for reimbursement. This employment attorney did not charge me for that call. Again, I could see God's favor on every turn.

One day, I ran into Leif's pastor — the same pastor who had brought the Pakistani student to me to purchase a car. He told me that he had been praying for me, that he knew I was a good man and that I was innocent – and that he knew Leif and how he operates. This touched me. Carrie's sense of justice was somewhat riled because she questioned, as she had many times before, why no one who supposedly knew about Leif and his dealings had ever done anything about it. It was enough for me that Leif's pastor knew the truth and was kind to me.

I once again had to look for a job. Now I had felony convictions on my record. I was likely locked into working in my home state, and there were not any manufacturing supervisor jobs available there. I applied for jobs throughout the United States and received a call from a company in Wisconsin. Again, through God's favor, I was offered a second-shift production supervisor position. I told the employer about my situation and he was very supportive.

In fact, my employer hires people who are on work release and believes in giving people another chance. Further, he stated that he would not do a background check. He would hire me immediately. I promptly went to discuss this with my parole officer to learn what my options were.

Carrie came with me and poured her heart out to the parole officer about the injustice, the corruption in the legal system, how the real criminal was still free and able to hurt more innocent people, and more. The parole officer was very kind and told us how she had gotten out of an abusive marriage and raised four children on her own. Life was tough, she told us. How we dealt with the pain was up to us – we could either harness the pain and learn and benefit from it, or become bitter and never get over it.

She said it was possible to work in Wisconsin. She would have to notify the parole office in Wisconsin and they could take over my case – with either positive or negative outcomes. This is because Wisconsin could be stricter in its treatment of me than where I currently was living. She also told us that she would be retiring in a year and that she would be recommending, in writing, that parole be terminated in a year.

When we left her office, I told Carrie, "My parole will be terminated before a year." She just looked at me, again, and didn't say anything.

Our eldest daughter, Änna, had graduated from college and had volunteered with Americorps for a year-long commitment as a Volunteer Coordinator with a non-profit social service agency in Washington,

D.C. She happened to be home visiting while all this was going on.

I decided to accept the job. I went to visit the parole officer again, but this time I took Änna with me. I told the officer that my lease for the home in that town was up that month and that I could not commute several hours each day to work. For the sake of my family, I believed we should move to the city where my new employer was based. She advised us again of the risk of moving and being under a Wisconsin parole officer. I told her that I would take that risk. As we left, I turned to Änna and said, "I will be released from parole in less than a year." Änna thought I was crazy and didn't say a word.

A week later, I visited the parole office. Carrie came with me. I had located a new home to lease, and I had written that address and the dates of my move on a piece of notepaper. We did not go to her office, but we spoke to her through the glass. I handed her the paper through the opening at the bottom of the glass and told her that I would be moving at the end of the week.

While Carrie was rejoicing at God's deliverance, she was still struggling with a lot of hurt and anger. The daughter of Shirley's close friend from Carrie's hometown was a Christian counselor and Carrie called to make an appointment. She explained to the receptionist that she grew up with the counselor and asked if it would be possible to see her. The receptionist told Carrie she would call her back. When the receptionist called back, she told Carrie she could get in the following week. Carrie went to see the counselor and poured out her heart. The counselor was very firm and said to Carrie, "What is the bottom line?" And then, through a series of questions the counselor asked, Carrie ultimately responded, "It's my pride." The counselor said, "Yes, it is your pride. And Carrie, it is all about Jesus. When you are angry and hurt, acknowledge the pain, release it to Jesus, and then leave it with Him." This was life-changing for Carrie. It was a hard word, as she was hoping for sympathy and participation in her pity party. Carrie is so thankful for God's wisdom through this counselor. And Carrie later learned that this counselor was booked more than a month out and the counselor did not send her a bill. God is so good!

Wisconsin

We packed and moved to Wisconsin the last week in April. We could see God's hand all over this, too. There were only three homes for lease in our new town. One was too small for our large family and was quite run down. The second had already been leased to someone and would be complicated to try to obtain. And the third was a large, immaculate home, custom-built by a former auto dealership owner and his wife. The husband had died, the wife was in a nursing home, the home had been on the market for some time, and the sons decided to rent it. Evidence of God's sense of humor was the back patio, where "Cadillac," "Chevy" and "Mazda" were inscribed in the surface of the floor, and a "Chevy" light hung in the basement over the pool table. Further, there was an entire room in the basement filled with collectible cars (which we promptly asked the owners to lock and to take the key with them as we didn't want our boys to discover this treasure).

After getting settled, we started looking for a church. We attended one church, but while Carrie felt at peace about it, I did not. We went back to our previous town, as Marina and Aisha were to participate in immersion water baptism at Living Word. A lady at Living Word, Marlene, asked if we had found a church. We told her, "No," and she told us about a woman pastor, Lynndene, at House of Prayer. Marlene said Lynndene was much anointed and that she loved to attend church there. Pastor Lynndene is good friends with Pastor Anderson, the former pastor of the church that Pastor John of Living Word had led after him. Marlene had attended Pastor Anderson's church and was now attending Pastor John's church and she had met Lynndene through Pastor Anderson. It is such a small world!

While Carrie had researched churches in our new town online and remembered reading about House of Prayer, she had not thought to visit it for some reason. She did recall leaving a message in response to a marriage retreat announcement, but had never received a call back. Carrie thanked Marlene. So the next Sunday, we attended House of Prayer. It was a small church, but I could sense God there immediately. Pastor Lynndene flows in the Spirit and clearly hears God's voice.

After the service, I told Carrie, "This is it. This is where I want to go to church."

One night in June, we were watching *It's Supernatural*. For some time, I had struggled with severe pain. My hip would get locked, forcing my right leg and foot to go far right, somewhat like a penguin. I had gone to the chiropractor several times and he would be able to unlock my hip (which would be very painful). After only one or two days, my hip would lock again. We were watching Sid Roth's program and his guest, Jim Richards. Mr. Richards prayed at the end of the program, and I prayed with him, placing my hand on my hip. I heard a pop and my hip snapped into place. I have not had any problems since. God is our healer today!

I received a telephone call in May from my parole officer, stating that I had moved without permission and that I had broken the law. I was beyond taken aback.

I had personally spoken to her, told her the dates I was moving, and had handed her the paper with my new Wisconsin address. It was beyond bizarre. I also received a letter stating I had violated parole.

The parole officer told me that she was retiring and that a new person was taking over. She said that she would have to notify the State of Wisconsin and that, because the nation-wide parole protocols had been violated, I would likely be remanded back to my former state. This would mean that I could no longer work in Wisconsin. I immediately thought of the year-long lease I had signed and wondered if I would able to break the lease without great financial repercussion.

Then I said, "God, now what? I need Your help and I know that You have a plan and that it will be good." I had no choice but to totally trust God. He had gotten me through thus far, and I knew that He could get me through the rest.

The parole officer told me that she would let her replacement know all the details. She said that I would be hearing from the new officer sometime soon. I did so. This officer told me that she believed the best route would be to contact the State's Attorney and the judge involved, and ask them to release me from parole as the release order would have to be signed by them both. She told me that she did not think there was even a 1 percent chance of this being successful. However, she would run it by her supervisor and get back to me. She told me that if it didn't work, we would have to return to her state. The head of the parole office gave his permission and a letter was sent to the State's Attorney and judge. I thanked God that He was in charge and that it was all good.

Jesus Christ In Person

ᕙ

On June 24, 2012, between 3 and 3:30 a.m., I had fallen asleep in my chair in the living room. Suddenly, I was somewhere else. The next thing I knew, I was standing in front of Jesus. I could feel the softest grass I had ever experienced under my feet. Jesus was surrounded by a beautiful, bright blue sky (I could not see a sun), red and yellow flowers, white butterflies, and to Jesus' right, water and mist and the sound of a waterfall.

Jesus is a beautiful man, very strong and well built with broad shoulders. He was not smiling and was not upset either. He was about 6'2" or 6'3" and was solidly built — approximately 240 to 250 pounds (I am 6' and it seemed that Jesus was a couple inches taller than me). Jesus had dark brown, almost black hair, brown eyes, and very thick eyebrows. His beard and mustache were beautiful and were close to His face and very neat; and they stopped at the top of His neck (they were not unkempt). His hair was wavy and came to above His shoulders. His hair followed the shape of His head and was not too curly. Jesus did not have light around Him on the outside of Him, but rather I could almost see through Jesus because of the brightness IN Jesus, which enhanced His color. It appeared that light was coming from inside Jesus, similar to a lighted globe. His lips appeared redder, if this makes sense. His skin was brown — about the same darkness of mine. He was wearing a white robe that stopped approximately two inches above his ankles. He also had a plain brown scarf over his shoulders that hung down and reached below the white robe in the back. He was wearing sandals similar to flip-flops. There was a wide band crossing over the top of Jesus' feet and the fabric was similar to unbleached linen or maybe burlap. The shoes looked hand-made, and while the linen crossed over Jesus' feet where the nail holes were, the light shone through the holes and the fabric so the holes were visible under the linen straps. I could see Jesus' left heel as well. The holes were visible in Jesus' palms and were approximately the size of my index finger — so quite large. The holes were not smooth, round holes, but rather somewhat jagged, although completely healed over.

Jesus was approximately four to five feet away from me. He raised His right arm and His arm was approximately two feet away from me. When He moved His arm, I could feel a refreshing breeze. At the same time Jesus raised His arm, I started feeling pain. It felt like it went on for an hour and in slow motion as Jesus' arm went up with His fingers open, not tight together. His sleeves hung down approximately six to eight inches from His wrists. Jesus, with His right arm outstretched and His palm open facing upward, spoke to me with a voice that was heavy and strong and said, "I need you." I felt weak and like I was going to drop down, but with effort stayed standing.

I responded, "Jesus, what do you need me for?"

Jesus said, "The world is coming to an end very soon and I need you."

I had so many questions, but I didn't ask Jesus because I didn't know if I had died and gone to Heaven or if I was alive, and I was struggling to stay standing.

I suddenly woke up. I immediately thanked God for being alive. It took me quite some time to get upstairs to bed. I had to hang on to the stair railing and drag myself up. I felt pain all over my body, my joints hurt, and I had a headache. I believe it is because of the power of being in God's presence and that Jesus' holiness and power were a lot for my physical body to withstand. When I awoke the next day, I still felt the aching in my joints and head, but I declared, "I'm healed," and after one day I felt better, other than a slight headache. I did not tell Carrie about the experience until Monday afternoon. However, when I came to bed around 4 a.m., I was clammy, shaking, and struggled to catch my breath. Carrie immediately thought "heart attack" and was concerned, but I told her that I wasn't feeling well, was exhausted, but that it was NOT a heart issue.

When I told Carrie about this experience, she remembered hearing about a young girl who had visions and had painted Christ. She ran to the computer and located the portrait of Jesus, *Prince of Peace,* by

Akiane Krimarik. Carrie asked me if the Jesus I saw and spoke with looked like Akiane's painting. I told her that the painting is 99 percent accurate. The only difference between Akiane's painting and Jesus is the color of His eyes. His eyes appeared dark brown to me, but Akiane used a greenish color for His eyes in her painting.

Visitations and Visions

⁂

S ince this experience, I have been clearly and audibly hearing Jesus speak to me about many things. I've been told to pray for specific people with specific names and health issues. I was shown a four-year-old girl named Sarah. She had cancer and had been through chemo, so she had no hair, but a gap in her front teeth when she smiled. God told me that her parents were alcoholics.

Jesus also wakes me up and tells me to read a certain part of the Bible. Prior to Christmas, He told me to read the book of Luke. Prior to that, He had told me to read 1 and 2 Corinthians. He also told me to read Hebrews.

After this experience, I began to see either light or darkness, and sometimes even demons in people. I could see these things in my employees at work. I would start each work night (I work from 4:30 p.m. to 4:30 a.m.) with prayer for my employers, for my employees, for our machines, and would claim that we would meet our production goals. I won't go into details, but there was a very negative atmosphere on my shift and there were many problems. One night, three machines went down at once, and I asked, "God, what is going on?" Then I remembered that I didn't pray that night. I immediately prayed, turned it over to the Lord, and we were able to meet our production goals.

After some time at my new job, employees began to trust me and to come to me with personal problems. I would talk with them, and have even prayed with a few of them. In one situation, a young man returned to his girlfriend and their son and proposed. They are marrying soon. In another situation, a woman's father, who was expected to die because he needed a kidney transplant, steadily improved, and was released from the hospital to go home. He is now stabilized.

Jesus told me that He wanted me to accept Him before my financial problems hit because He wanted me under His wing and protection, due to the gravity and seriousness of what I would be facing. If I were not a Christian, He would not have been able to move on my behalf. Because I accepted Him, I was in Christ, and He could deal with me as a Christian.

*****

After midnight on Saturday, June 30, 2012, I suddenly woke up, told Carrie "Balsam, I mean Psalm 108," and went back to sleep.

Carrie couldn't sleep after this, and as she loves to track breaking news and news as it relates to prophecy, she was looking at news headlines and saw that Yitzhak Shamir had just died. The scripture I had been given by God directly related to what Yitzhak Shamir had stood for throughout his life – to not give up the land of Israel. After becoming a Christian, I was miraculously delivered from my hatred of Israel. Carrie and I had Jewish friends and I had never hated Jews as individual people, but I did feel hatred toward Israel and its government. When I accepted Christ, I immediately became a defender of the nation of Israel. One of my favorite programs is *The Hal Lindsey Report.* Prior to accepting Christ, I would get furious when Carrie would listen to his program. This, again, is miraculous and part of being a new creature in Christ.

*****

On July 26, 2012, I received a call from my parole officer. I was driving to work, recognized the number on my cell phone, and did not feel emotionally strong enough to take the call. The officer left a message and I listened to it.

She said, "Congratulations! You are released from parole immediately. We will be sending you a letter." I called her right away, and she told me, "In my twenty-two years of serving as a parole officer, I have never witnessed someone being released from parole after only four months. It's a miracle."

Yes, another miracle from my great God. He is certainly able to do above all that we ask or think! And God's timing is impeccable. I was released from parole nearly one year to the day after the first newspaper article came out. Our steps are surely ordered of the Lord. He cares about every detail, and the timing is further proof that only God could orchestrate such dates. These were not coincidences!

I prayed for Carrie's mother because she did not have an appetite. Her appetite increased and she has been eating continually every since. She even wakes up in the middle of the night to eat.

*****

On July 29, 2012, I woke up and heard Jesus audibly tell me, "You need to talk to your brother Nabil about me."

I said, "Lord, you know how hard that's going to be."

He said, "It won't be, look at him." He then showed me a vision of my brother Nabil standing in our cousin's house in Jordan, and my brother was telling him, "Come to Jesus." I have not yet shared my conversion with this brother, as he and his wife are conservative Muslims. They watch Islamic programming and adhere to strict Islamic dress. They see everything in black and white. I know that I must share with this brother, but I have been praying for Jesus to give me the opportunity at the right time. In particular, my children love their

239

cousins very much and I believe that this brother and his wife will cut off all communication with our family when I tell them. Carrie is very close to this sister-in-law, and it will be very hurtful if our families no longer spend time with one another. I know it will be very difficult, but I am not afraid because Jesus is with me.

Later that morning, I attended church at House of Prayer. Pastor Lynndene's five-point sermon was about one's vocation being worship, about trusting God no matter what, about being rooted like a tree and bearing fruit, and about being in faith. This confirmed 100 percent what I had been telling Carrie and her parents in conversation the day before. Every point I brought up to my family on Saturday was confirmed on Sunday by Pastor Lynndene.

*****

On July 30, 2012, I met with Pastor Lynndene and shared my testimony. She told me that I am a forerunner in the last days and will lead in battle. She said that I am a standard bearer and an example. She shared that I will not fit with other Christians. She told me that

I was chosen before I was born for God's purposes, not mine. She said that I walk in signs and wonders, in part because of my genealogy as a child of Abraham (Arabs and Jews). She said that, in the Word, it says that Greeks come to Christ through knowledge and Jews come to Christ through signs. She said that God has been working with signs and wonders throughout my lifetime and with my wife. She said that Muslims are having visions and that all Christians should live supernaturally.

*****

On August 3, 2012, I attended a Holy Spirit conference at a Lutheran church in a city suburb where I heard Bill Davis, a former convict, give his testimony. It was a great encouragement to me. I also heard Jesus audibly say, "Make a DVD of your testimony."

*****

On August 4, 2012, I heard Jesus say, "You need to start preaching."

*****

On August 5, 2012, Jesus spoke to me while sitting in Pastor Lynndene's Sunday church service. In Arabic, He said, "I am here in this church." Typically Jesus speaks to me in English. This is the first time He spoke to me in Arabic.

*****

On August 6, 2012, I heard that the name of the ministry should be "Max In Christ Ministry," and the logo should be a white flag with a dove and a tear coming from the dove's eye. I saw myself in a suit, giving my testimony, and behind me was a background of blue, red and white. I contacted Carrie's cousin who has a graphic design business, and he has created the logo and the website.

Jesus appears to me regularly and tells me to pray for certain people with certain issues. I have recorded them in a notebook, but am not including them here as they were specific words for specific people. These are people I do not know and have never met. Jesus tells me what is needed, I pray in faith, and that is that. I don't know if I will ever have an opportunity to meet these people, but I would sure like to if God ordains it.

*****

On August 12, 2012, Pastor Lynndene prophesied over me for approximately fifteen minutes. She said, "God has you on a fast track for His plans and purposes. Many will envy; they have not paid the price. You did not have a choice yet you stood faithful."

*****

On August 28, 2012, I was awakened at 6:15 a.m., and God said, "Jerusalem will be okay in sixty-five days."

I said, "It is good to hear from You, Lord," and Jesus said, "It's good to hear you, too." I could see Jesus' face.

Sixty-five days from this date was November 2, 2012. Jerusalem was okay on this day and I don't know if something evil planned for that day was thwarted, but that is the word I received.

*****

On September 1, 2012, I saw the following flashing numbers, "1, 2, 3, 4, 5." I thought this was in connection with the sixty-five-day countdown.

*****

On September 2, 2012, Pastor Lynndene gave me a word that even the birds would carry my message where it should go.

*****

On September 7, 2012, I received a word that there would be a tornado in the U.S. the next day. There was a tornado in New York the next day.

*****

On September 10, 2012, while I was sleeping, Jesus talked to me and told me about how much He loves His children. He brought up the young people who use drugs and meth and who struggle with addictions. He said, "I love them so much and I want them to live in peace and in faith and to turn to God. I can't save them unless they surrender to Me and believe that what they are doing is wrong."

I said to Him, "They don't know any better. But You love them so much; they are Your children."

He said, "I love them so much and it's just like the generations before. I've been dealing with this all my life. Every generation has these addictions and it is getting worse and worse."

Then I said, "Lord, Your people need a wake-up call and I will be working on getting more kids to come to You. I'm going to do my best to get as many as I can."

He said, "I just love them so much and I want as many as possible of my children in my kingdom. I want them all." At the end, I saw that Jesus was smiling at me.

*****

On September 17, 2012, Jesus told me to write a book. The cover should have a blue sky on it and the title, across the top, should be *Live in Faith*. This book is my obedience to Jesus' directive.

*****

On September 29, 2012, I was awakened at 4:00 a.m. and told to pray for people to forgive one another: fathers, mothers, sons, daughters, aunts, uncles, grandparents; families must forgive one another and love one another.

*****

On November 7, 2012, Carrie went to Wednesday prayer meeting at church. Pastor Lynndene's friend, a former pastor, was visiting from a nearby city. He gave Carrie the word, "As of today, you are free! Your children have been a heavy burden on you; it will be okay. There is an anointing on your life, a prayer anointing. It is the beginning of a ministry. Control is broken. You have been under terrible attack and the attacks are now over. God loves you."

*****

In October, my father had fallen and broken his hip while getting up from the table after eating dinner. He lives with my brother Bassem and his family. Based on the way the family described the scenario to me, I believe my father had a stroke and then subsequently fell. He was in the hospital and then was moved to a nursing home. While in the hospital he was doing amazingly well and was putting forth effort toward recovery.

Once he was moved to the nursing home, he stopped progressing and started regressing. He would not eat or make any attempt to walk. He started seeing people who had passed away years ago and he would have conversations with them. While we knew some of the medication could cause hallucinations, it was more than just the medication. I believed that my father was going to pass away imminently.

Carrie went to Wednesday night prayer and shared with Pastor Lynndene and the women there how much she loved my dad and desired that he would be saved. One of the women who was faithful to pray, Terri, saw a picture of Jesus on a slide and she told Carrie, "Jesus is just going to slide right into your father-in-law's heart."

When I came home to eat at 10:30 p.m. that night, Carrie told me about this and we decided that when I got off work in the morning at 4:30 a.m., we would immediately drive to the nursing home and pray for my father and his salvation. We had not been able to have any alone time with him or talk with him about salvation because my family kept a nearly twenty-four-hour vigil around my dad. My sister had flown from Jordan to stay with him and one of my brothers, my sister-in-law, or my niece and nephews would stay with my dad at all times. The only time he was alone was in the middle of the night and the early morning.

On December 6, 2012, Carrie and I arrived in his room and he was in and out of sleep. The room was very dark. Carrie prayed in the Spirit and I laid hands on my father and prayed for him. My hands became very hot and I felt God's physical hand on me, as I often do when I pray for healing for people. I prayed for maybe ten or fifteen minutes. A light shone by my father and this was clearly the Lord, because he was in a darkened room. He had a roommate and the roommate was next to the window and there were curtains separating the neighbor's bed from my father's bed. It was definitely a supernatural light.

I heard Jesus say, "Your dad will be with Me. It will be days."

Carrie and I left, I told her what I had heard, and we both believed that my father was going to die within days. Instead, my sister called later that day to say that my father had walked forty steps, had gone up stairs, and had eaten two meals. She and my brother were told that there were two strangers in my father's room early in the morning and they were perplexed as to who had visited my father. Then I told them that my wife and I had been with him. My father steadily progressed after that and was released within a week to go home with my brother. He is probably doing better physically now than he was prior to his fall, in that he has quit smoking and as a result, now has a healthy appetite. All glory to God!

This experience taught me that interpretation is very important. I interpreted Jesus saying, "It will be days," to mean days until my father's death. Rather, it was days until my father's recovery. I am learning to pray and ask God for His interpretation of things I am shown. I am still in the learning process.

*****

On December 29, 2012, Jesus told me, "Whoever is saved will be with Me and whoever is not saved will not be with Me."

*****

On December 31, 2012, Jesus spoke to me and said, ". . .It is coming to an end."

*****

On January 4, 2013, I had another visitation. I was in the sky with Jesus. There was a strong, wild wind and Jesus' hair and robe were blowing about. We were above Jerusalem and Jerusalem was okay, but all the countries around Israel were on fire. The Dead Sea was flooding into the Jordan River (possible shaking of the earth). Then we were above the U.S. Half of the U.S.

disappeared under the ocean; the divide went from the west to the east. I could see buildings collapsing and then going under. Other buildings fell and hit adjacent buildings. I believe I was seeing a shifting of the plates on a worldwide scale. The first area I saw go under was California and it went east quickly and north more slowly. Afterwards, less than half of the U.S. remained. People and bodies were flying, cars were hitting people, buildings, and other cars. Some areas had mountains sheared in half, with people on the mountain crying for help and the other half of the mountain in the sea. Planes were crashing. There were islands where land was surrounded by water in the areas of the U.S. that had not fallen into the sea. (Minnesota had pockets of water and land.) It was a shaking of the earth. North America was cut in half; the rest of the world was on fire. The remaining part of the U.S. and Canada experienced earthquakes and fire. I thought that parts of Oregon and Washington were okay, and Iowa, and Nebraska. I could see the White House and a wall of water rushing behind it and around it and crashing through the windows. But I believe Texas, Louisiana, Florida, and the Carolinas were totally gone. And I was surprised because many major Christian ministries are headquartered in these areas.

As all this horror was taking place, our nation's leadership was running way. I couldn't hear anything and I was high in the sky, yet I could see details close up. I could see the shock and horror on people's faces. Then I saw government leaders (the current administration's family, Clintons, British royals, former presidents Bush and more) boarding a ship/submarine on the East Coast.

Jesus said, ". . .My people will be saved and will be in a better place today (referring to the Christians who were not part of the privileged elite boarding the vessel.)"

I could hardly stand because of the wind. I was in the sky, looking down, about four to five feet from Jesus. I asked, "Jesus, what about my family?" Jesus said, "They will be fine." I woke up sick and felt ill for five days, and I was more tired than usual for two weeks.

*****

On January 13, 2013, at 3:45 a.m., I had a vision. I saw Paul in jail behind bars — huge, rusty, roughly hewn bars. Paul was short with dark hair and black eyes and almost chubby. His clothing was like the Romans' (a beige/brown robe with a dark brown, maybe black fabric going around his waist and shoulders). Paul told me how strong he (Paul) was in the Lord. He said that he went through terrible things and he knew he would get through them because he (Paul) trusted in God no matter what. He told me that there are so many Jews who don't believe him, but Jesus does; Jesus knows the truth. Paul told me that he knew he would be free, even though those around him were saying otherwise. Then I saw Paul in an area with olive trees and grape vines and there were four or five angels around him. Paul told me that I (Muhannad) was sitting on Jesus' feet, "You are so close to Jesus; you are sitting on his feet." Then he gave me Hebrews 6:17 and 18:

[17]Because God wanted to make the unchanging nature of his purpose very clear to the heirs of what was promised, he confirmed it with an oath.[18]God did this so that, by two unchangeable things in

which it is impossible for God to lie, we who have fled to take hold of the hope set before us may be greatly encouraged (NIV).

*****

On January 17, 2013, I saw what I believe was Iran. There was smoke coming from buildings, shooting, gunfire, and flames everywhere. People were running in the streets and women were covering their heads and shouting, "Allahu Akhbar" which means "God is great".

*****

I had e-mailed my story to the *It's Supernatural* web site, and one of Sid Roth's staff members contacted me and suggested that I come to Charlotte, North Carolina, for a taping of the show. David gave us money for airfare and we traveled to Charlotte for the January 24 taping. We arrived in Charlotte several hours before taping, and I went inside to confirm that we had tickets. The woman in charge of the seating was there. She had assigned us to the overflow seating and I told her that I wanted to sit right in front of Sid. She then told me that she would put us in the third row. When we arrived at the taping that night, we were able to sit in the front row – right in front of Sid Roth. And the two individuals he interviewed had amazing testimonies. While we were not able to speak with Mr. Roth, I was able to give his assistant my story and a CD of my testimony. I have been communicating with a staff person from this ministry since that time.

The next day, a major ice storm was predicted. Carrie asked that we stop at the Billy Graham Evangelistic Association headquarters, and she was able to meet with her former boss who was scheduled to retire in April of this year. It was a very special time for her. She had worked with this man when she returned from Jordan after marrying me.

*****

On January 28, I woke up at 4:45 a.m. when I heard Jesus' voice say, "You are My Father's friend, just like Abraham."

I asked, "What do you mean, God's friend like Abraham?"

He said, "In faith."

I asked, "Explain to me what you mean by 'like Abraham in faith.'"

Jesus said, "James 2."

James 2:23 reads, ". . .Abraham believed God, and it was imputed unto him for righteousness: and he was called the Friend of God."

Later that day, our family friend, Agnes, called and said, "I believe that John 15:15 is for you." John 15:15 reads, "[15] I no longer call you servants, because a servant does not know his master's business. Instead, I have called you friends, for everything that I learned from my Father I have made known to you" (NIV).

*****

One night recently, I was at work, and one of my employees injured his hand. I took him to the Emergency Room and the ER doctor took x-rays. He told my employee that his thumb was fractured, that it would require a pin, and that he would not be able to bend his thumb ever again.

I left the employee in the ER to wait for the surgeon's arrival in the morning. I went home and prayed for this man. I asked God for total and complete healing. My employee called me today to say that when the surgeon arrived from a neighboring city, the surgeon said, "Your thumb is not fractured." My employee received eight or nine stitches and will be completely fine.

*****

On February 27, 2013, my body was asleep in bed, but I was awake. Jesus appeared to me. We were sitting on a tall building, maybe somewhere in the Twin Cities, possibly the IDS building. The weather was nice and I was wearing short sleeves. There was a clear sky and a nice breeze. It was maybe June or July. Jesus was wearing a white gown and He had a little smile.

Jesus said, "My people need to stop looking at material things and need to focus on their faith and coming to Me."

I asked Him, "What do You mean about material things?"

He said, "My people are looking for material things in their life. I want them to come to Me, in stronger faith, because what I showed you before is coming very soon."

I said, "What do You mean, what You showed me before?"

He said, "The time I showed you the earth shaking and the land cracking open (the vision He gave me before.)."

I asked, "How soon, Lord?"

He replied, "Years of your life are days for Me."

I said, "What do You mean?"

He said, "It will be very, very soon."

Essentially, people are focusing on their lifestyle and not on God. Then Carrie woke me up.

*****

On Tuesday morning, February 19, 2013, I was in my chair. I saw Jesus standing across from the garden at the White House. He said, "Look at the White House Secret Service."

I said, "It looks beautiful in Washington, D.C., this morning."

Jesus said, "Look at the Secret Service. Half of them are not human. They are cloning them in the Pentagon in order to protect the President." I asked Him why. He said that this was being done because many humans disagree with the President's policies and clones will not argue or dissent – they will obey.

*****

Sunday, March 3, 2013:

I was sitting in church, and Pastor and the congregation were praying in the Spirit. I heard Jesus talk to me in my right ear. He said, "Tell them to have faith and believe in Me and tell them that I need My people with Me. I need all My believers to be with Me."

Then Pastor said, "Someone here has a word from the Lord. Don't hold back; please come up and share, whoever you are."

I walked up to the front and said, "The Lord spoke to me and He wants me to tell you that the end is coming soon and He wants His believers with Him." While I was talking, I felt Jesus' arm on my shoulder and I could hardly breathe or get my words out.

Jesus told me, "It's going to be days." Days to Jesus are years to us. "Tell everybody in this church that I love them so much. And everybody in this church will be with Me."

Life In Christ

꩜

After receiving Christ, there was an immediate change in the atmosphere of our home. It was no longer taboo to speak the name of Jesus. Soon we were praying together before every meal. This was revolutionary, as there was an unspoken rule that if we prayed before we ate, it was "Bismillah rahman rahim," "In the name of God, the Most Gracious, the Most Merciful," not thanking and blessing the food in Jesus' name.

Whereas the younger children were hungry and open to Jesus Christ, Marina had grown up under the oppression of fear as to what could and could not be said regarding Christianity. She remembers her mother praying with her and whispering, "Don't ever say the name of Jesus out loud or your father will get angry."

She remembers how Christmas decorating and celebrating were at first allowed at a minimum, but then taken away completely. She remembers how a picture of Jesus based on the Shroud of Turin that Carrie's parents had given her in high school sat in storage, as it was not allowed to be hung on the wall. Marina had many conflicting emotions and, at best, was oblivious to religion, at worst, sullen and suspicious of religion.

Because of the many struggles Marina was dealing with as a young person, trying to find herself, and made more complicated because of the tensions in our home, she went through many difficult circumstances. As Carrie continued to go to church at Living Word prior to my salvation, Kristine would build and encourage Marina. Marina grew to love attending youth group, and a major reason for this was Kristine's continuous love and support for Marina, no matter how many mistakes she had made. Kristine offered her the unconditional love of Christ. Another woman there, Cheryl, also encouraged and supported Marina and found any opportunity to show her love.

Carrie would tell Änna about the changes happening in our home, but Änna was skeptical. While Änna and I had gone through many power struggles, we loved and respected one another. Yet Änna had lived the typical American life at college, questioning her faith and participating in the lifestyle that has become standard for today's youth. She was a good person, but she was not living a Christian lifestyle; she was not in relationship with Jesus.

Änna left for Washington, D.C., and would come home only to visit. Each time she did, she could physically sense and feel the changes in our home. She witnessed the family prayer at meal times and the Christian programming we were soaking in. Most of all, she saw God work miracles in my legal battle and my release from parole after only four months. She began to believe that my salvation was real and that Jesus is still alive and working miracles today.

As Jesus began revealing Himself to me by audibly speaking to me, through visions and more, Änna almost seemed frightened at first, as if this was simply too much, too bizarre to comprehend and handle. Carrie would tell her, "Dad heard something." Änna would respond, "What did Dad hear now, Mom?" Carrie would tell her, Änna would laugh and say, "It is just so different, everything is so different." But she has seen over time that what God tells me comes to pass and she is open to God's leading.

After moving to Wisconsin, Marina continued to struggle. The Holy Spirit would alert me to things that were happening with Marina. For example, He would tell me to go to her room in the middle of the night, just as she was preparing to sneak out. Or, when talking with Marina about a poor decision, Jesus would tell me exactly what Marina was thinking in her head, and I would be able to tell Marina, "You are thinking this," and Marina would say to me, "Dad – How did you know that is exactly what I was saying in my head?" I would tell her, "Jesus told me because He loves you and He wants me to help you." The Holy Spirit has allowed me to stop Marina from certain decisions on several occasions by alerting me ahead of time. Marina recognizes this and is learning that it is better to be honest, because she will be found out if she is not up front.

Soon after moving to Wisconsin, Marina had a frightening scare. She was walking in the kitchen and suddenly passed out, falling on the floor in a heap. Her face was flushed and she experienced numbness in her feet and hands and they had turned blue. Carrie panicked and wanted to call the ambulance. Marina came to and I took her into the dining room and began to pray. I spoke healing over her and thanked Jesus that Marina was healed. The numbness quickly went away, her color came back, and she was fine. Marina recognized that Jesus' healing was hers and she received it.

Marina was blown away by an offer from Cheryl at Living Word to take her senior pictures. Marina traveled there and Cheryl spent many hours with her, taking photos throughout the city at some of Marina's favorite locations. Cheryl even took pictures of Marina with her beloved dog, Finn. The love and support that continues to be extended to us, even after moving from that town and from Living Word, is a testimony to that congregation's love for Christ and for others.

Änna surprised us all by making the decision to leave her salaried position in Washington, D.C., and move to Wisconsin for the summer to learn organic farming. Änna and I have had a number of conversations and I try to exhort her to pray and follow the Lord's leading. She does clearly hear from the Lord, but she is not yet fully surrendered to Him. She still loves Israel and hopes to return there, preferably in a capacity where she is able to work and stay for some time. I believe she has a unique call on her life, as she is a Palestinian-American who grew up in a Muslim household that is now living for Christ. She has a cultural and religious understanding that is unique among many. And she has witnessed miracles herself, so she knows that God is real and that He cares about the minutest details of her life.

For example, Änna is not into material possessions. She is much like her father, Barhoum. She loves life and people, and she is perfectly happy and willing to give away anything and everything. But she has one special possession, a ring she purchased when living in Israel that is inscribed in Hebrew. She called Carrie one day, very upset, because the ring had fallen off her hand while she was walking home from work in Washington, D.C. She had looked all over the sidewalk and road for the ring and was unable to find it. She returned to the spot later and looked again, to no avail. She looked through her bags and her clothing—nothing. Carrie told her, "I will pray. The Bible tells us that everything hidden shall be revealed and that, when we speak the Word, the angels must obey." Many hours later, Änna called Carrie. She was very excited. She said, "Mom, you would never believe what happened! I was sitting on the floor in my room (Änna's room was in the attic of the house she shared with other Americorp roommates) and the ring flew in the air and landed in front of me!" God is good, He is faithful, and He cares about the things that are important to us.

Jesus has told me that both Änna and Marina are not yet in relationship with Him. I continue to live my life for Christ and I believe that they both will come to Christ. The Word says in Proverbs 22:6, "Start children off on the way they should go, and even when they are old they will not turn from it" (NIV). God is faithful and I trust Him in this matter.

Aisha is full of joy and loves the Lord. While she loved her youth group and leaders at Living Word and was growing and thriving there, she has struggled since moving to Wisconsin. She often expresses how much she misses her Living Word church family. In fact, after moving to Wisconsin, Living Word graciously and generously sponsored Aisha so she could attend

Bible camp. Aisha received the gift of the Holy Spirit while there. While Aisha is very social and has made many friends in Wisconsin, she has not been growing spiritually as she could. This is further complicated by the fact that I work nights and am simply not home with my family like I should be. I believe this will change in the near future, as God wants the best for me and my family, and working the shift that I do is not healthy for my children.

Sayf always had a soft heart towards the Lord. He was very open and receptive to Christ as a little boy. He loves history and he loves to write. As his teacher told him last year, "You have a powerful voice," in reference to his writing. He is very happy and content just dreaming or creating military battles with marbles or pencils. He also loves to play outdoors and enjoys his rip stick. When he was younger, Sayf would often ask Carrie questions about God and about creation and about how things work, and she would explain what she could, all the while trying not to tell him too much as she didn't want to make me angry should I hear Sayf mention Jesus. When I accepted Christ and expressed my desire to be baptized, Sayf quickly asked to be baptized with me. Because Sayf is very sensitive, he is very tender. I believe I need to be home when the family is awake so I can be more involved with teaching and mentoring him. He loves video games, and because this became out of balance through my legal battle and our moves, we are working to correct this.

According to my brothers, Sami is just like me. He is rambunctious and full of energy. He moves through our home like a whirlwind. Sami also loves to pray. At meal times, he prays first and then I pray. Sami loves Jesus and loves to draw pictures of Jesus. Just this Easter, he ran to his room, grabbed paper and markers, and drew a picture of his grandparents' home with Jesus on the cross in front of it, encircled in a heart. He asks many questions about Jesus, about heaven, and about this world. He also has many pretend battles with his play swords. He once told Carrie, "Mom, I will never die because I have the Word, the sword of faith, and God protects me!" If he feels ill, he asks us to pray for him and receives his healing. Recently, Carrie had a stomachache and happened to mention it out loud. Sami came to her, laid hands on her, and prayed. Carrie felt heat from his hands and the pain went away.

Our children love their cousins, Nabil's children, and look forward to time spent with them with great anticipation. The boys, especially, have many questions after visiting their cousins. For example, Sami told us last week, "I'm half Muslim." I told him, "You are half Arab." The boys look up to and want to be like their cousins.

We are teaching our children, as Jesus told me, that the only thing blocking people from healing and from receiving all that God has for them is their fear. If people come to Christ in complete trust and faith, healing is there for them. Fear blocks and complete trust brings flow and breakthrough. I often tell Carrie, "Just believe and receive. It is that simple." Carrie tries to explain to me that, while it is simple, human nature fights against this and fear can have a powerful grip. But I reiterate, "Jesus says to believe and receive." We believe that the first thing to do when battles come is to go to the Lord. We desire to teach our children to walk in faith in every area, from the little things to the big things. The more they walk out their faith over small issues, the more their faith will be built up to handle major issues.

Carrie's uncle in Indiana, the same uncle who had boldly shared Christ with me through the years, invited me to speak at three churches in his area. He is currently a chaplain and he also serves as a pastor. He made all the arrangements, gave me books from his extensive library, and he and his wife graciously hosted me, Carrie, and her parents in his home. This is another miracle and a testament to seeds sown. While it may take many years to see results, God is faithful. I'm so thankful to this uncle and aunt for the love they showed me over the years, even when I was not receptive to their message of Christ.

I shared my salvation with one brother, Bassem. He was accepting and supportive of me, in part because our brother Barhoum shared his salvation with Bassem before he died. Bassem has had years to ponder this. In addition, Bassem is married to a born again Christian, so he is more open to Christ than my other family members. He is very concerned and worried about how the rest of my family will respond to my conversion. At the same time, he believes it will be fine after they have time to process it. Meanwhile, I continue to pray for Bassem's salvation and I believe he will come to Christ.

Recently, Jesus audibly told me, "You didn't get married to Carrie because of Änna. You married Carrie because she needed you."

In closing, we believe that Videll's word to Carrie is coming to pass. While Carrie and I had three daughters with light brown hair, not blonde hair, we had three daughters first, followed by two sons. We believe that we are living in the last days and will be working side by side in the end time harvest. Perhaps the relationship with Barhoum was out of God's will, but God's grace and mercy allows for Plan B and C when we, in our humanness, walk away from Plan A. We have seen that God does not waste any experience, no matter how painful, and how important it is to believe Him, trust Him no matter what in every situation, and simply live in faith.

This is my testimony until now. Jesus has told me that time is short, that He loves people so much, and that He desires relationship with them. There is much harvesting to be done in these last days.

Bible Verses Carrie Quoted Nearly Daily When Standing for my Deliverance in the Legal Battle

*All verses are taken from the book, *Scripture Keys for Kingdom Living,* compiled by June Newman Davis, Missionary Evangelist, Eighth Printing 1987. R. R. Donnelley and Sons Co.

**Those verses that were especially meaningful at the time are in bold.

Heb. 4:12

For the Word of God is quick, and powerful, and sharper than any two-edged sword, piercing even to the dividing asunder of soul and spirit, and of the joints and marrow, and is a discerner of the thoughts and intents of the heart.

Rev. 12:11a

And they (Christians) overcame him (Satan) by the blood of the Lamb, and by the Word of their testimony; . . .

Num. 23:19

God is not a man, that He should lie; neither the son of man, that He should repent; hath He said, and shall He not do it? Or hath He spoken, and shall He not make it good?

Ps. 107:20

He sent His Word, and healed them, and delivered them from their destructions.

Ps. 119:130

The entrance of Thy Words giveth light; it giveth understanding unto the simple.

Prov. 30:5

Every Word of God is pure: He is a shield unto them that put their trust in Him.

Isa. 43:26a

Put me in remembrance: . . . (of His Word!)

Jn. 14:26

But the Comforter, which is the Holy Ghost . . . shall teach you all things, and bring all things to your remembrance, . . .

Jas. 1:5

If any of you lack wisdom, let him ask of God, that giveth to all men liberally, and upbraideth not; and it shall be given him.

Jas. 3:17

But the wisdom that is from above is first pure, then peaceable, gentle, and easy to be entreated, full of mercy and good fruits, without partiality, and without hypocrisy.

1 Jn. 2:27

But the anointing which ye have received of him abideth in you, and ye need not that any man teach you: but as the anointing teacheth you of all things, and is truth, and is no lie, and even as it hath taught you, ye shall abide in Him.

Mt. 6:10

Thy kingdom come. Thy will be done in earth as it is in heaven.

Mt. 15:28

. . .O woman, great is thy faith; be it unto thee even as thou wilt.

Prov. 1:23

. . . I will pour out My Spirit unto you, I will make known My Words unto you.

1 Jn. 5:14-15

And this is the confidence that we have in Him, that, if we ask any thing according to His will, He heareth us: (Eph. 3:20) And if we know that He hear us, whatsoever we ask, we know that we have the petitions that we desired of Him.

Isa. 1:19

If ye be willing and obedient, ye shall eat the good of the land:

1 Thes. 5:16-18

Rejoice evermore. Pray without ceasing. In every thing give thanks: for this is the will of God in Christ Jesus concerning you.

Ps. 55:18

He hath delivered my soul in peace from the battle that was against me:. . .

Ps. 25:2

O my God, I trust in thee: let me not be ashamed, let not mine enemies triumph over me.

Ps. 37:3-5

Trust in the Lord, and do good; so shalt thou dwell in the land, and verily, thou shalt be fed. Delight thyself also in the Lord; and He shall give thee the desires of thine heart. Commit thy way unto the Lord; trust also in Him; and He shall bring it to pass.

Ps. 91:4

He shall cover thee with His feathers, and under His wings shalt thou trust: His trust shall be thy shield and buckler.

Col. 2:14

God blots out even the proof against us, nailing it to His Son's cross.

Jn. 3:17

For God sent not his Son into the world to condemn the world; but that the world through him might be saved.

Rom. 1:16

For I am not ashamed of the gospel of Christ: for it is the power of God unto salvation to every one that believeth; to the Jew first, and also to the Greek.

Heb. 1:14

Are they not all ministering spirits, sent forth to minister for them who shall be heirs of salvation?

Ps. 84:11b

No good thing will He withhold from them that walk uprightly.

Isa. 59:19b

. . .When the enemy shall come in like a flood, the Spirit of the Lord shall lift up a standard against him.

Rom. 8:37

. . .in all these things we are more than conquerors through Him that loved us.

2 Thes. 3:3

But the Lord is faithful, who shall stablish you, and keep you from evil.

Ps. 31:19-20

Oh how great is Thy goodness, which Thou hast laid up for them that fear Thee; which Thou hast

wrought for them that trust in Thee. . .Thou shalt hide them in the secret of Thy presence. . .Thou shalt keep them secretly in a pavilion. . .

Ps. 91:9-11

Because thou hast made the Lord, which is my refuge, even the most High, thy habitation; There shall no evil befall thee, neither shall any plague come nigh thy dwelling. For He shall give his angels charge over thee, to keep thee in all thy ways.

Ps. 119:116-117

Uphold me according to Thy Word, that I may live: . . . Hold thou me up, and I shall be safe: . . .

Ps. 121:8

The Lord shall preserve thy going out and thy coming in from this time forth, and even for evermore.

Prov. 1:33

But whoso hearkeneth unto Me shall dwell safely, and shall be quiet from fear of evil.

Prov. 3:25-26

Be not afraid of sudden fear, neither of the desolation of the wicked, when it cometh. For the Lord shall be thy confidence, and shall keep thy foot from being taken.

Josh. 1:8

This book of the Law shall not depart out of thy mouth; but thou shalt meditate therein day and night, . . .then thou shalt make thy way prosperous, and then thou shalt have good success.

Prov. 8:21

That I may cause those that love me to inherit substance; and I will fill their treasures.

Isa. 48:17b

. . .I am the Lord thy God which teacheth thee to profit, which leadeth thee by the way that thou shouldest go.

Isa. 55:11

So shall My Word be that goeth forth out of My mouth: it shall not return unto Me void, . . .and it shall prosper in the thing whereto I sent it.

281

Phil. 4:6

Be careful for nothing; but in every thing by prayer and supplication WITH THANKSGIVING let your requests be made known unto God.

1 Thes. 5:18

In every thing give thanks: for this is the will of God in Christ Jesus concerning you.

Heb. 13:15

By Him therefore let us offer the sacrifice of praise to God continually, that is, the fruit of our lips giving thanks to His name.

1 Pet. 2:9

But ye are a chosen generation, a royal priesthood, an holy nation, a peculiar people; that ye should shew forth the praises of Him who hath called you out of darkness into His marvelous light:

Isa. 26:3

Thou wilt keep him in perfect peace, whose mind is stayed on Thee: because he trusteth in Thee.

2 Thes. 3:16

Now the Lord of peace Himself give you peace always by all means. The Lord be with you all.

Heb. 12:1b

. . .let us lay aside every weight, and the sin which doth so easily beset us, and let us run with patience the race that is set before us,

Jas. 1:2-3

My brethren, count it all joy when ye fall into divers temptations; Knowing this, that the trying of your faith worketh patience.

THROUGH THE BLOOD OF JESUS, THE SON OF GOD, THE DEVIL HAS NO PLACE IN ME, NO POWER OVER ME, BECAUSE OF ALL THAT JESUS DID FOR ME ON THE CROSS!

Isa. 61:3

. . .to give unto them. . .the garment of praise for the spirit of heaviness. . .that He might be glorified.

Rom. 8:1

There is therefore now no condemnation to them which are in Christ Jesus, who walk not after the flesh, but after the Spirit.

Ps. 34:7

The angel of the Lord encampeth round about them that fear Him, and delivereth them.

Ps. 46:5

God is in the midst of her; she shall not be moved: God shall help her, and that right early.

Ps. 68:19

Blessed be the Lord, who daily loadest us with benefits, even the God of our salvation.

Ps. 147:3

He healeth the broken in heart, and bindeth up their wounds.

1 Jn. 4:4b

. . .greater is He that is in you, than he (devil) that is in the world.

Ps. 46:1

God is our refuge and strength, a very present help in trouble.

1 Cor. 14:33

For God is not the author of confusion, but of peace, . . .

Ps. 71:1

In thee, O Lord, do I put my trust: let me never be put to confusion.

Isa. 50:7

For the Lord God will help me; therefore shall I not be confounded: therefore have I set my face like a flint, and I know that I shall not be ashamed.

Jn. 8:36

If the Son therefore shall make you free, ye shall be free indeed.

Jn. 10:10b

. . .I am come that they might have life, and that they might have it more abundantly.

1 Cor. 2:16b

. . .But we have the mind of Christ.

1 Cor. 6:17

But he that is joined unto the Lord is one Spirit.

2 Cor. 3:17

Now the Lord is that Spirit: and where the Spirit of the Lord is, there is liberty.

2 Cor. 10:5b

. . .bringing into captivity every thought to the obedience of Christ;

Phil. 4:19

But my God shall supply all your need according to His riches in glory. . .

Eph. 2:14

For He is our peace, who hath made both one, and hath broken down the middle wall of partition between us;

Ps. 145:30

The Lord preserveth all them that love Him:. . .

Prov. 3:11-12

My son, despise not the chastening of the Lord; neither be weary of his correction: For whom the Lord loveth he correcteth; even as a father the son in whom he delighteth.

Isa. 38:17

Behold, for peace I had great bitterness; but thou hast in love to my soul delivereth it from the pit of corruption: for thou hast cast all my sins behind Thy back.

Jer. 31:3

. . .Yea, I have loved thee with an everlasting love: therefore with loving kindness have I drawn thee.

Jn. 3:16

For God so loved the world, that he gave his only begotten Son, that whosoever believeth in him should not perish, but have everlasting life.

Rom. 8:37

Nay, in all these things we are more than conquerors through him that loved us.

Eph. 2:4, 6

But God, who is rich in mercy, for his great love wherewith he loved us, . . . hath raised us up together, and made us sit together in heavenly places in Christ Jesus:

Phil. 1:6

Being confident of this very thing, that he which hath begun a good work in you will perform it until the day of Jesus Christ:

1 Jn. 4:9-11

In this was manifested the love of God toward us, because that God sent his only begotten Son into

the world, that we might live through him. Herein is love, not that we loved God, but that he loved us, and sent his Son to be the propitiation for our sins. Beloved, if God so loved us, we ought also to love one another.

Jn. 15:12

This is my commandment, that ye love one another, as I have loved you.

Gal. 5:13b-15

. . .by love serve one another. For all the law is fulfilled in one word, even in this; Thou shalt love thy neighbor as thyself. But if ye bite and devour one another, take heed that ye be not consumed one of another.

Eph. 4:32

And be ye kind one to another, tenderhearted, forgiving one another, even as God for Christ's sake hath forgiven you.

1 Thes. 3:12-13

And the Lord make you to increase and abound IN LOVE ONE TOWARD ANOTHER, and toward all men, even as we do toward you: To the end he may stablish your hearts unblameable in holiness before God, even our Father, at the coming of our Lord Jesus Christ with all his saints.

Mt. 10:26b

. . .for there is nothing covered, that shall not be revealed; and hid, that shall not be known.

1 Cor. 2:10

. . .but God hath revealed them unto us by His Spirit. . .

Lu. 8:17

For nothing is secret, that shall not be made manifest; neither any thing hid, that shall not be known and come abroad.

Ps. 37:24

Though he fall, he shall not be utterly cast down: for the Lord upholdeth him with His hand.

Ps. 73:23

Nevertheless I am continually with thee: Thou hast holden me by my right hand.

Ps. 121:8

The Lord shall preserve thy going out and thy coming in from this time forth, and even for evermore.

Isa. 45:2

I will go before thee, and make the crooked places straight: I will break in pieces the gates of brass, and cut in sunder the bars of iron:

Ex. 33:14-15

. . .My presence shall go with thee, and I will give thee rest.

Ps. 5:12

For thou, Lord, wilt bless the righteous; with favor wilt thou compass him as with a shield.

Ps. 125:2

As the mountains are round about Jerusalem, so the Word is round about His people from henceforth even forever. (Round about you – as a shield)

Isa. 52:12

And I will put My spirit within you, and cause you to walk in My statutes, and ye shall keep My judgments, and do them.

Mt. 28:20b

. . .lo, I am with you always, even unto the end of the world.

Eph. 4:31-32

Let all bitterness, and wrath, and anger, and clamour, and evil speaking, be put away from you, with all malice: And be ye kind one to another, tenderhearted, forgiving one another, even as God for Christ's sake hath forgiven you.

Isa 55:7

Let the wicked forsake his way, and the unrighteous man his thoughts: and let him return unto the Lord, and He will have mercy upon him; and to our God, for He will abundantly pardon.

Mk. 11:25-26

And when ye stand praying, forgive, if ye have ought against any: that your Father also which is in heaven may forgive you your trespasses. . .

Mal. 3:16-18

Then they that feared the Lord spake often one to another: and the Lord hearkened, and heard it, and a book of remembrance was written before him for them that feared the Lord, and that thought upon his name. AND THEY SHALL BE MINE, SAITH THE LORD OF HOSTS, IN THAT DAY WHEN I MAKE UP MY JEWELS; AND I WILL SPARE THEM, AS A MAN SPARETH HIS OWN SON THAT SERVETH HIM. THEN SHALL YE RETURN, AND DISCERN BETWEEN THE RIGHTEOUS AND THE WICKED,

BETWEEN HIM THAT SERVETH GOD AND HIM THAT SERVETH HIM NOT.

Mal. 4:2

But unto you that fear my name shall the Sun of righteousness arise with HEALING IN HIS WINGS; AND YE SHALL GO FORTH, AND GROW UP AS CALVES OF THE STALL.

Ps. 34:9

Oh fear the Lord, ye his saints: for THERE IS NO WANT TO THEM THAT FEAR HIM.

Ps. 34:10

The young lions do lack, and suffer hunger: but they that seek the Lord SHALL NOT WANT ANY GOOD THING.

Ps. 145:19

He will fulfill the desire of them that fear Him: He also will hear their cry, and will save them.

Ps. 147:11

The Lord taketh pleasure in them that fear Him, in those that hope in His mercy.

Ps. 31:19-20

Oh how great is thy goodness, which thou hast laid up for them that fear thee; which thou hast wrought for them that trust in thee before the sons of men! **THOU SHALT HIDE THEM IN THE SECRET OF THY PRESENCE FROM THE PRIDE OF MAN: THOU SHALT KEEP THEM SECRETLY IN A PAVILION FROM THE STRIFE OF TONGUES.**

Ps. 56:11

In God have I put my trust: I will not be afraid what man can do unto me.

Isa. 51:7

Hearken unto me, ye that know righteousness, the people in whose heart is my law; fear ye not the reproach of men, neither be ye afraid of their reviling.

Heb. 13:6

So that we may boldly say, The Lord is my helper, and I will not fear what man shall do unto me.

Deut. 31:8

And the Lord, He it is that doth go before thee; He will be with thee, He will not fail thee, neither forsake thee: FEAR NOT, NEITHER BE DISMAYED.

Ps. 34:4

I sought the Lord, and He heard me, and delivered me from all my fears.

Ps. 91:5

Thou shalt not be afraid for the terror by night; nor for the arrow that flieth by day;

Prov. 18:10

The Name of the Lord is a strong tower: the righteous runneth into it, and is safe.

Mt. 28:20

. . .lo, I am with you always, even unto the end of the world.

2 Thes. 3:3

But the Lord is faithful, who shall stablish you, and keep you from evil.

2 Tim. 1:7

For God hath not given us the spirit of fear; but of power, and of love, and of a sound mind.

Heb. 1:14

Are they not all ministering spirits, sent forth to minister for them WHO SHALL BE HEIRS OF SALVATION?

Ps. 21:2

Thou hast given him his heart's desire, and hast not withholden the request of his lips.

Ps. 103:17

But the mercy of the Lord is from everlasting to ever-lasting upon them that fear Him, and His righteousness unto children's children;

Isa. 54:13

And all thy children shall be taught of the Lord; and great shall be the peace of thy children.

Heb. 4:14

Seeing then that we have a great high priest, that is passed into the heavens, Jesus the Son of God, let us hold fast our profession.

Heb. 10:23

Let us hold fast the profession of our faith WITHOUT WAVERING: (for He is faithful that promised;) EVERY PROMISE IN THE WORD OF GOD!

Mt. 21:21

. . .Verily I say unto you, If ye have faith, and doubt not, ye shall not only do this which is done to the

fig tree, but also if ye shall say unto this mountain, Be thou removed. . .it shall be done.

1 Cor. 2:5

That your faith should not stand in the wisdom of men, but in the power of God.

Heb. 11:1

Now faith is the substance of things hoped for, the evidence of things not seen.

Heb. 11:6

But without faith it is impossible to please him: for he that cometh to God must believe that He is, and that He is a rewarder of them that diligently seek Him.

Deut. 31:6, 8

Be strong and of a good courage, fear not, nor be afraid of them: for the Lord thy God, he it is that doth go with thee; He will not fail thee, nor forsake thee. . .

Mt. 6:33

But seek ye first the Kingdom of God, and His righteous-ness; and all these things shall be added unto you.

Phil 1:6

Being confident of this very thing, that He which hath begun a good work in you will perform it until the day of Jesus Christ:

Phil 4:6

Be careful for nothing; but in EVERYTHING by prayer and supplication with thanksgiving let your request be made known unto God.

Ps. 107:2

Let the redeemed of the Lord SAY SO, whom He hath redeemed from the hand of the enemy;

Ex. 15:6

Thy right hand, O Lord, is become glorious in power: Thy right hand, O Lord, hath dashed in pieces the enemy.

Ps. 34:19

Many are the afflictions of the righteous: but the Lord delivereth him out of them all.

Ps. 55:16-18

As for me, I will call upon God; and the Lord will save me. . .He shall hear my voice. He hath delivered my soul in peace from the battle that was against me: for there were many with me.

Ps. 91:3

Surely He shall deliver thee from the snare of the fowler, and from the noisome pestilence.

Ps. 107:6

Then they cried unto the Lord in their trouble, and He delivered them out of their distresses.

Ps. 143:11

Quicken me, O Lord, for Thy name's sake: for Thy righteousness' sake bring my soul out of trouble.

Ps. 144:7

Send Thine hand from above: rid me, and deliver me out of great waters,. . .

Prov. 11:8

The righteous is delivered out of trouble, and the wicked cometh in his stead.

Isa. 33:2

O Lord, be gracious unto us; we have waited for Thee: be Thou their arm every morning, our salvation also in the time of trouble.

Jer. 15:21

And I will deliver thee out of the hand of the wicked, and I will redeem thee out of the hand of the terrible.

Joel 2:32

Whosoever shall call on the name of the Lord shall be delivered:

Jn. 8:32

And ye shall know the truth, and the truth shall make you free.

Lk. 10:18

Jesus said, "Behold, I give unto you power to tread on serpents and scorpions, and over all the power of the enemy: and nothing shall by any means harm you."

Col. 1:13

Who hath (past tense) delivered us (believers) from the power of darkness, and hath translated us into the kingdom of His dear Son.

Eccl. 12:11

The words of the wise are as goads, and as nails fastened by the masters of assemblies, which are given from one shepherd.

1 Cor. 4:5

Therefore judge nothing before the time, until the Lord come, who both will bring to light the hidden

things of darkness, and will make manifest the counsels of the hearts: and then shall every man have praise of God.

Ps. 33:10

The Lord bringeth the counsel of the heathen to nought: He maketh the devices of the people of non effect.

Isa. 55:7

Let the wicked forsake his way, and the unrighteous man his thoughts: and let him return unto the Lord, and He will have mercy upon him; and to our God, for He will abundantly pardon.

Prov. 28:13

He that covereth his sins shall not prosper: but whoso confesseth and forsaketh them shall have mercy.

Ps. 34:18

The Lord is nigh unto them that are of a broken heart; and saveth such as be of a contrite spirit.

Jer. 31:13

. . .for I will turn their mourning into joy, and will comfort them, and make them rejoice from their sorrow.

Josh. 1:8

This book of the law shall not depart out of thy mouth; but thou shalt meditate therein day and night, that thou mayest observe to do according to all that is written therein: for then thou SHALT MAKE THY WAY PROSPEROUS, and THEN THOU SHALT HAVE GOOD SUCCESS.

Ps. 35:27B

. . .Let the Lord be magnified, which hath pleasure in the prosperity of His servant.

Ps. 46:1

God is our refuge and strength, a very present help in trouble.

Ps. 55:22

Cast thy burden upon the Lord, and He shall sustain thee: He shall never suffer the righteous to be moved.

Isa. 41:13

For I the Lord thy God will hold thy right hand, saying unto thee, Fear not; I will help thee.

Phil. 4:19

But my God shall supply ALL your need according to His riches in glory by Christ Jesus.

3 Jn. 2

Beloved, I wish above all things that thou mayest prosper and be in health, even as thy soul prospereth.

Recipes

Mensaf

<u>Meat for Mensaf</u>

3 to 5 lbs. lamb pieces

4 chicken breasts or legs, remove skin

2 lemons, cut in half or fourths

canola oil

3 T. salt

peppercorns, small handful

10 cardamom pods, crushed

3 t. cardamom, crushed/powder

10 cloves, whole

4 bay leaves, ripped in half

2 to 3 cinnamon sticks

allspice (to be sprinkled on meat after it has been cooked)

Cut lemon in half; squeeze and rub on bottom and sides of deep kettle or pot. Heat canola oil; add lamb and braise. Add hot water to nearly top of pan; add spices and salt. Cut other lemon half into fourths and add to water. Add the cinnamon sticks and peppercorns. Skim scum from meat, returning any spices that were in the scum back to the pot.

In a separate pot, not as large, repeat the process for the chicken.

When the meat is cooked and tender, remove from stock and cool. Shred the meat, removing all bones and skin, if any. Sprinkle with 1 to 2 t. allspice.

Rice for Mensaf

approximately 12 c. stock from lamb and chicken
approximately 6 c. rice
1 stick butter
salt to taste (approximately 1 T.)

½ to 1 t. turmeric ½ to 1 t. cumin

1 t. seven spices mix*

1 t. cardamom, ground/powder

If 12 cups stock from meat, then 6 c. rice (Use Uncle Ben's or Egyptian rice). Add butter to the stock. Add all spices. When the water is almost the same level as the rice, cover the pot. Cook over medium heat and allow steam to collect 5 to 10 minutes, then turn to low.

*If seven spices mix is not available in one's area, it is possible to make it at home.

Seven Spices

2 T. ground black pepper

2 T. paprika

2 T. ground cumin

1 T. ground coriander

1 T. ground cloves

1 t. ground nutmeg

1 t. ground cinnamon

½ t. ground cardamom

Mix all ingredients well. Store in an airtight container or in freezer. You can also roast and grind these spices yourself first before mixing.

Yogurt Sauce

2 16 oz. containers yogurt, plain

2 16 oz. containers sour cream

½ spoon turmeric

1 to 2 T. Crisco, butter flavored

1 T. canola

lamb and chicken stock

*It is important to stir the below mixture in one direction only.

Stir until free of lumps and very smooth. Add enough lamb and chicken stock to make a mixture that is more thin than thick. Stir in the Crisco and canola oil. Add salt. Heat on low, gradually raising the temperature until the yogurt boils (there should be separate drips from the spoon). Separate into 2 containers.

Nuts

½ to 1 c. pine nuts

½ to 1 c. almonds, skins removed

½ to 1 c. pistachios

1 to 2 T. oil

3 to 4 c. boiling water

Boil almonds for a few minutes, soak in water, and remove the skins. Soak all nuts in water until expanded. Heat canola; brown pine nuts first, then almonds, and finish with pistachios. When the nuts are golden brown, remove them from the oil and set aside.

Putting Mensaf Together

Place large, thin bread on bottom of a large tray. If this bread is not available, use fillo dough that has been broiled until it is light brown. Spoon the rice over the bread, leaving room around the edges. Cover the rice entirely with shredded chicken and chunks of lamb. Cover with browned nuts. Spoon the yogurt sauce from one container onto the rice. Pour the yogurt sauce from the remaining container into a pitcher and serve on the side so people can add more sauce if they would like.

Maklouba or Upside Down

1 chicken, cut in pieces and skinned

or use chicken breasts

5 to 6 potatoes

1 head cauliflower, cut into med. florets

3 to 4 tomatoes, sliced

4 c. rice, Egyptian

2 large blocks chicken bouillon

1 T. salt

2 to 3 t. seven spices

corn oil

3 to 4 T. butter or oil

Soak chicken for 30 minutes or so in ¼ to ½ c. lemon juice, onion cut in fourths, 1 T. salt, 1 t. pepper, 1 t. seven spices and a little water. Pat dry. Fry chicken in corn oil until brown and remove. Soak rice in warm water for 20 minutes. Peel, slice and fry potatoes in oil chicken was fried in and remove when golden brown.

Fry cauliflower until golden brown and remove. Melt butter or oil in bottom of deep kettle or pot. Sprinkle with a little rice, approximately ¼ c. Place tomatoes over rice. Layer the potatoes, cauliflower and meat over the rice. Rinse rice that has been soaking and place on top of vegetables. Dissolve two chicken bouillon in 1 c. hot water, pour over rice. Pour seven cups boiling water mixed with salt and seven spices over the rice. Bring to a boil, turn to low. After 20 to 30 minutes, when rice is tender, turn upside down. Serve with yogurt on the side.

Addas Soup

2 c. red lentils

8 c. water/broth

½ to 1 t. cumin

½ t. turmeric and/or paprika

1 large onion, diced

1 to 2 potatoes, cubed

2 cloves garlic, minced

2 T. olive oil

2 bouillon cubes

1 lemon, juiced

salt and pepper to taste

1 to 2 carrots, sliced

Wash lentils. Add broth, potatoes and carrots and bring to boil; lower heat and simmer for 30 minutes. Stir occasionally. When lentils are tender, add spices and bouillon. Sauté onion and garlic in oil, when brown add to soup. Simmer five minutes. Turn off heat and add lemon juice.

Falafel

1 can chick peas, drained

2 cloves garlic

1 onion

3 to 4 t. parsley, freshly chopped

1 egg

3 t. falafel spice mix

2 ½ to 3 t. salt

½ to 1 t. pepper

8 T. bulgur, cracked wheat, soaked 1 hour and drained

½ to 1 c. flour

vegetable oil for frying

pita bread for serving

Place first 8 ingredients in food processor and process until smooth. Add bulgur and process until it forms a large ball. Add ½ to1 c. flour until the mix holds its form but it should not be so thick that it is like bread dough. Heat oil to 375 degrees and drop mixture into hot oil using a meatball scoop or otherwise form into balls and drop into hot oil. Fry until crisp and dark brown. Remove with slotted spoon and drain on paper towels. Serve in pita pockets with tahini sauce or serve with humus dip.

Kinafa

1 box kinafa dough, frozen

8 oz. sweet white cheese, shredded

1 T. butter Crisco, melted

1 can kashta/puck cream

2 sticks butter, melted

¾ c. sugar

1 lb. ricotta cheese

¼ c. pistachios, chopped

½ to ¾ block cream cheese

Syrup

2 c. sugar

1 T. orange blossom water

1 ½ c. water

2 to 4 drops lemon juice, freshly squeezed

Prepare syrup first. Mix lemon, sugar and water together in a small saucepan. Bring to a boil and simmer for 9 minutes. Remove from heat and add orange blossom water. Return to heat and let bubble for a minute. Remove from heat.

In a large bowl, break kinafa dough into small, fine pieces. It is preferable to do this while the dough is still frozen or partially frozen as it will break easily. Once it thaws, it is difficult to break into pieces. Add melted butter Crisco and butter and, by hand, work the butter mixture into the dough until it is totally absorbed. Place a layer of dough on a large, circular tray or pan that has been greased well.* Mix the cheeses and cream together well. Spoon on top of dough and spread to within ½ inch of the edge. Top with remaining dough. Bake at 400 degrees F for 30 to 40 minutes, until golden brown. If you prefer the top to be a deeper brown, broil for one to two minutes, watching it every second to make sure it does not get too brown or burn. Sprinkle with pistachios and pour cooled syrup over the kinafa while it is still hot.

*Make sure the pan can fit inside the oven.

Basbousa

½ c. unsalted butter

1 t. baking powder

1 t. vanilla

½ t. baking soda

2 eggs

¾ c. yogurt

2 c. fine semolina

almonds, blanched and slivered

½ to 1 c. coconut, optional

One syrup recipe.

Cream the butter, sugar and vanilla until light and fluffy. Add the eggs, one at a time and beat well. Sift the semolina, baking powder and soda. Fold into butter mixture alternately with yogurt. Pour batter into a small round and greased baking pan. Garnish with almonds. Bake at 400 degrees for 30 minutes. Pour one recipe of cooled syrup over the hot cake and let the cake cool thoroughly. Cut into diamond shapes and serve cold.

Kafta

2 lbs. fine ground lean beef or lamb

2 to 3 t. salt

2 small onions, minced

½ t. pepper

1 c. finely chopped parsley

½ t. cinnamon

2 tomatoes, diced

¼ t. allspice

Mix all ingredients together. Press and flatten into large tray or plan. Cover with sliced tomatoes or with partially cooked sliced potatoes (peeled, sliced and boiled for 15 minutes). One may also cover with tahini sauce, especially if using potatoes on top.

Tahini Sauce

1 clove garlic, minced

½ c. water

1 t. salt

½ c. lemon juice

½ c. tahini

Mash garlic and salt. Add tahini, mixing well. Gradually add water, blending thoroughly. Add lemon juice and blend well. Pour over meat and bake.

Bake at 400 degrees for 35 to 40 minutes.